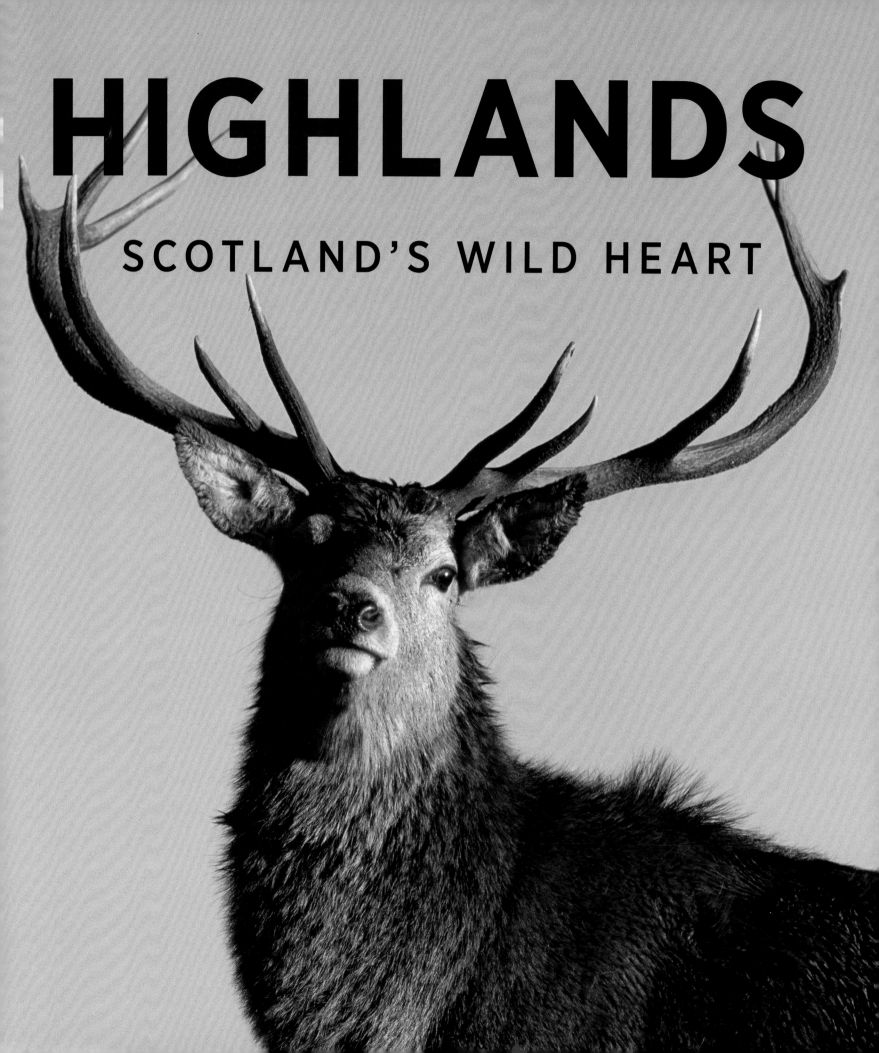

HIGHLANDS

SCOTLAND'S WILD HEART

HIGHLANDS
SCOTLAND'S WILD HEART

As seen on the
BBC

STEPHEN MOSS
Photographs by Laurie Campbell

BLOOMSBURY

LONDON · NEW DELHI · NEW YORK · SYDNEY

Dedication

To Lucy and John Lister-Kaye, my dear friends in the Highlands.

Bloomsbury Publishing Plc

50 Bedford Square   1385 Broadway
London   New York
WC1B 3DP   NY 10018
UK   USA

www.bloomsbury.com

BLOOMSBURY and the Diana logo are trademarks of Bloomsbury Publishing Plc

First published 2016

British Library Cataloguing-in-Publication Data

A catalogue record for this book is available from the British Library.

Library of Congress Cataloguing-in-Publication data has been applied for.

ISBN: HB: 978-1-4729-1900-7
       PB: 978-1-4729-1901-4
       ePub: 978-1-4729-1902-1

2 4 6 8 10 9 7 5 3 1

Design by Nimbus Design

Printed and bound in China by C & C Offset Co. Ltd.

To find out more about our authors and books visit www.bloomsbury.com. Here you will find extracts,
author interviews, details of forthcoming events and the option to sign up for our newsletters.

CONTENTS

Introduction 8

Winter into Spring 10

Spring into Summer 72

Summer into Autumn 152

Autumn into Winter 210

Acknowledgements 268

Further reading 269

Index 270

INTRODUCTION

Of all Britain's wild places, surely none are so beautiful, so scenic, and so special as the Scottish Highlands. Stretching across hundreds of square miles, the exact definition of the region is hard to establish: it includes the Inner Hebrides, but not always the outer isles; Orkney, but definitely not Shetland; as well as the Cairngorm plateau, the valleys of Speyside and Deeside, the Flow Country, Ben Nevis, and the Great Glen.

But the Highlands are about far more than geography: they are also a state of mind. The very name speaks of wildness and wilderness, of towering mountains and deep glens, of fast-flowing rivers and rocky coasts, and above all, of some of Britain's most extraordinary and spectacular plants and animals.

Not that Highland wildlife is always easy to see. The place gives up its secrets unwillingly at times, and effort, hard work and a fair amount of luck are needed to see some of the more elusive wild creatures. But what wild creatures! Golden Eagle and Bottlenose Dolphin, Pine Marten and Osprey, Reindeer and Red Deer, Black Grouse and Red Squirrel, Ptarmigan and Capercaillie, the Atlantic Salmon and the rare and well hidden Scottish Wildcat, are just a few of the iconic species found here, some found nowhere else in Britain. They are accompanied by a fabulous supporting cast of birds and mammals, reptiles and amphibians, butterflies and dragonflies and, during the spring and summer, stunning displays of wild flowers.

The Scottish Highlands change not just season by season but also day by day; but in this book I have chosen – as in the accompanying BBC TV series – to focus on the transformations that take place, slowly but surely, over the course of a calendar year. The book is divided into four seasons, each of which is a transition in itself: from winter to spring, spring to summer, summer into autumn and finally autumn back to winter, as the natural year comes full circle once again. It is a story of hardship and opportunity, of wonder and surprise, and above all of how nature finds a way in even the harshest of conditions.

In between the stories of the wild creatures that make their home in this glorious part of the world, there are profiles of some of the many people who have chosen to live alongside the wildlife here. They love the Highlands as, if you have already been here, you will easily understand. If you haven't been yet, this book is an invitation to visit, and to experience the wonders of Scotland's wild heart for yourself. You'll be glad you did!

Stephen Moss

Winter into Spring

WINTER ON THE HIGH TOPS

The Reindeer herd trudges through the deep, crisp snow, heading towards the distant summit of the mountain. An icy wind cuts through the chill January air, while a glowering grey sky occasionally erupts with flurries of flakes; little miracles of nature, each unique hexagonal fragment of snow drifting down to join millions of others on the ground.

All around, a sea of white, broken only by the occasional grey boulder, the huge, jagged outline of the mountain itself and these sturdy, patient animals – perfectly adapted to this Arctic scene.

Yet this is not Lapland, but the Cairngorm plateau in the Highlands of Scotland. At 57 degrees north, more than 1,000 km (620 miles) south of the Arctic Circle, this place is a long way from the Reindeer's normal home. For the Reindeer is a true Arctic animal, perfectly adapted to life on the barren, frozen tundra of Scandinavia and Siberia, and across the huge expanses of Alaska and Canada, where the species is known as Caribou. So what on earth are these animals doing here?

The story of the Cairngorm Reindeer herd goes back more than 60 years, to 1952, the year that Queen Elizabeth II came to the throne, and to a visionary man named Mikel Utsi, a Swedish Reindeer herder. He and his wife, Dr Ethel Lindgren, brought eight animals across the North Sea to Scotland, and put them in a fenced enclosure near Aviemore, before eventually releasing them on the slopes of Cairn Gorm. Later, more Reindeer were brought over, and today there are around 150 animals living a semi-feral lifestyle here.

Of all the animals you might expect to encounter in the Scottish Highlands, the Reindeer is one of the least expected, yet also one of the most appropriate. It is not usually considered to be a native British animal, yet it has perfectly good credentials to be regarded as one. Less than 10,000 years ago, towards the end of the last ice age, wild Reindeer roamed all over Britain as far south as Kent. Although this may seem a long time ago in our human history of these islands, it is but a blink of an eye in geological and natural history terms.

The Cairngorm Reindeer have lived on the mountain for more than 60 years, since being brought here from Sweden.

The Reindeer's story reminds us that wild creatures have always come and gone from the Highlands, and that what we see today is only a snapshot of the wildlife that has lived here in the past, and what might be found here in the future.

Watching the Reindeer as they amble across this windswept landscape makes us realise just how well adapted they are to what is surely the most hostile environment in Britain. Their fur is made up of two layers: a thick, woolly undercoat, covered with a layer of longer, tightly packed hairs, which are hollow and filled with air – helping the animal to retain its precious body heat even in sub-zero temperatures and cold winds.

The Reindeer's hooves are also adapted to living in very different conditions from season to season. In spring and summer Reindeer have sponge-like pads to enable their feet to gain traction on boggy ground, but in autumn these shrink to allow the rim of the hoof a better grip on slippery snow and ice.

Reindeer even breathe differently from other mammals: their nostrils have a very large internal surface area, which enables them to warm the chilly air before it enters their lungs, thus ensuring that they retain as much body heat as possible.

Most extraordinary of all, as Reindeer walk across the snow-covered plateau their lower legs make a loud clicking sound, produced by a tendon in the animal's foot slipping across the bone. This is a very energy-efficient way of keeping the herd together when the animals have their heads down to graze, or during bad weather, when visibility may be very poor.

At this time of year in their native home, Reindeer mainly feed on lichens, especially one particular species know as Reindeer Moss. Surviving on such a meagre, low-energy food is nothing short of incredible – and the Reindeer is the only mammal species to do so.

Reindeer also feed on grasses, sedges, willow and birch leaves, as well as fungi and even the occasional bird's egg. However, for much of the year they survive only on the lichen, which they dig out from under the snow using their specially adapted hooves. In fact, the Cairngorm Reindeer have a relatively easy life. They are regularly given supplementary food, a daily event that allows visitors to get a really close look at these splendid animals.

Not all the wild creatures here on the high tops are quite as lucky: for them, winter is the toughest season of all, a season during which they must work hard to survive in order to breed during the coming spring and summer. The story of how they do so is filled with drama and surprise.

Reindeer are brilliantly adapted to life in a cold, snowy environment, with a thick coat to keep them warm even when the temperature drops well below freezing.

Cairngorm weather and climate

Way south of the Arctic Circle this place may be, but the Cairngorm plateau is nevertheless an example of what scientists call an Arctic-Alpine ecosystem, because of its high altitude.

Although the actual figures vary depending on the weather conditions, a rough rule of thumb is that for every 150–170 m (490–550 ft) rise in altitude, the average temperature drops by about 1.8 °C (3.2 °F). So here, at 1,000–1,300 m (3,300–4,200 ft) above sea level, the average temperature is 11–16 °C (20–29 °F) lower than at the coast. This is before taking into account aspects such as the wind-chill factor, which can make conditions on the high tops feel far colder.

The weather here can be unforgiving for both human and animal life. The summit of Cairn Gorm itself saw the strongest gust of wind ever recorded in the British Isles: an incredible 276 km (173 miles) per hour, on 20 March 1986. To the south, the town of Braemar also holds the record for the lowest temperature ever recorded, –27.2 °C (–17 °F). This occurred not just once, but twice, in February 1895 and again in January 1982.

So despite the plateau's relatively southerly latitude, the climate here is far more similar to that of locations well to the north, such as southern Greenland, Iceland, Scandinavia and Arctic Russia. The wildlife is not exactly the same due to geographical differences and the fact that we are an island. Nonetheless, there are many plants and animals here that might otherwise only be expected to be seen in the High Arctic.

CREATURES OF THE SNOW

The high tops of the Scottish Highlands are not easy places in which to live. As a result, only a handful of creatures manage to survive here all year round. To do so they must adapt to a whole new world: the white blanket of snow that dominates the landscape throughout the winter months, and indeed often well into the spring.

Three creatures – two species of mammal and one bird – have adapted to the coming of the snow in the best possible way, by changing the colour of their fur or feathers from browns and greys to white.

The Ptarmigan, Mountain Hare and Stoat are the real tough guys of Britain's wildlife. For in winter, at a time when virtually every other species has either headed down the mountains towards the lowlands or the coast, or has travelled even further away, migrating vast distances to spend the winter in southern Europe or Africa, these three have chosen to stay put. It's a risky strategy but a clever one, for one thing is sure: the resources – in terms of food and shelter – may be thin and meagre, but if a creature can manage to stay here all year round it will face little competition.

On New Year's Day a visitor to the high tops could be forgiven for wondering why any wild creature would choose to live in such a hostile environment, and at such a difficult time of year. With fewer than seven hours between sunrise and sunset, daylight is a precious resource, while average temperatures are generally below freezing, with a continuous bone-chilling wind usually blowing from the north or east.

The Highlands in winter are one of the harshest environments in Britain. Yet some wild creatures are tough enough to survive and even thrive here. These footprints were made by a Mountain Hare.

The Ptarmigan (top) and the Mountain Hare (bottom) are two of the toughest wild creatures in Britain, spending the whole of their lives on the high tops, whatever the weather.

To survive here at all, let alone thrive, you need to be perfectly adapted to the harsh environment – and these three species are certainly examples of that. Nevertheless, the first impression you get as you step off the funicular railway and begin the long walk south towards Ben Macdui is that there are no living creatures here at all.

Eventually, however, as you trudge across the snowy wastes, you hear a sound. It's a harsh, rapid croak, rather like that of a very loud and deep-voiced frog. You turn your head this way and that, trying to work out which direction the sound is coming from. Then you hear it again, even closer. Finally, as you step tentatively forwards across the snow, a movement catches your eye, and a tight little group of birds about the size of plump domestic chickens rockets across your path and lands a few metres away. It's a flock of Ptarmigan – one of the toughest birds in the world.

The name Ptarmigan (pronounced tar-mig-en, with a silent 'p') comes from an old Scots Gaelic word meaning 'croaker'. Alternative spellings include tarmachan, tarmagan and termigant – the 'p' at the front was added by the 17th-century Scottish ornithologist Sir Robert Sibbald, who mistakenly thought that the word had a Greek origin.

The Ptarmigan is the smallest and lightest of Britain's four species of grouse, yet it is also by far the toughest, for although Red Grouse live on the lower slopes of the Cairngorms all year round, they cannot survive on the high tops in the middle of winter.

Among Britain's birds the Ptarmigan is unique – the only species to have three distinct plumages during the course of the year. The birds are speckled brown in summer, which enables them to blend in with the heather, grey in the autumn to match the rocks and boulders, and snow white (apart from a black bill, eye-patch and outer-tail feathers) during the winter – and indeed often long into the spring, when snow still covers much of the ground.

As well as their change in appearance, Ptarmigan have developed several other adaptations to enable them to survive the cold winter months on the plateau. These include 'snowshoes': a dense layer of feathers on the soles of the feet, which enables them to stand for long periods on the snow or ice without their legs freezing.

Ptarmigan also add about one-third of their body weight in fat each autumn, in case there are long periods of bad weather when finding food can be difficult – if not impossible. Should this happen, a Ptarmigan buries itself in a snow hole where, surrounded by an insulating blanket of snow, it has a far better chance of surviving than if it stays out on the exposed mountainside. Finally, like Reindeer, Ptarmigan keep warm by having a dense layer of feathers – not fur – covering their body and enabling them to retain as much heat as possible, even when the temperature drops to well below freezing.

Ptarmigan generally feed by day, so as soon as dawn breaks, even before the weak winter sun has begun to rise, they head out of their night-time lair and begin to search for food. They use their powerful feet to move the snow aside to reach the vegetation beneath, finding lichen, heather and moss on which they feed.

As the sky gradually lightens and the Ptarmigan begin their brief day's foraging, another mountain creature is coming to the end of its feeding period. Mountain Hares are, like the Ptarmigan with which they share their home, perfectly adapted to living in this harsh environment. Although smaller and lighter than the more familiar and far more widespread Brown Hare, Mountain Hares are a lot tougher – indeed, they are the toughest of all our native wild mammals. Of

roughly 350,000 Mountain Hares in Britain, the vast majority live in Scotland, and one of their main strongholds is on the Cairngorm plateau.

Although you can come across Mountain Hares at any time of day, they are more active by night, when they are far safer from predators such as Stoats and Golden Eagles. In winter this gives them a huge advantage over the day-feeding Ptarmigan: with over 16 hours between dusk and dawn they have more than twice as much time to feed. Nevertheless, in such a harsh environment there can be no guarantee of survival.

Just like Ptarmigans, Mountain Hares are perfectly adapted to life in this cold, snowy and unforgiving place. They too change their colour, from grey-brown during the summer and autumn to white in winter, although unlike the Ptarmigan they do not turn wholly white, often showing a greyish wash across their upperparts and having black tips to their ears. Their feet have large, splayed toes – again, rather like snowshoes – so that they can walk or run across snow without sinking down into it.

Unlike the young of Brown Hares and Rabbits, Mountain Hare leverets are born with a covering of fur.

The Mountain Hare is the tough guy of the mammal world and, like the Ptarmigan, turns white in winter to stay camouflaged against predators such as the Golden Eagle.

Winter can be incredibly harsh for the wild creatures of the Highlands, as prolonged frost and snow make finding food difficult.

This is crucial if they are to survive, as some youngsters appear as early as March or April, when snow is usually still lying on the ground and night-time temperatures plummet way below freezing. At this time of year these usually solitary animals often come together to feed. Being in a group provides safety in numbers, as they are better able to spot predators and sound the alarm; it may also help them find better sources of food. Even so, life for a Mountain Hare is harsh, brutish and short: only 20 per cent of young hares survive their first year of life, and although they can live as long as ten years, many are taken by predators – such as the third member of our snow-adapted trio, the Stoat.

While the Mountain Hare and Ptarmigan are montane specialists confined to upland habitats, the Stoat is far more common and widespread throughout Britain. In some ways this makes its presence here, and its adaptation to life on the high tops, even more remarkable. Whereas in the rest of Britain the Stoat keeps its typical chestnut-and-white coat all year round, here in the Highlands it undergoes a remarkable transformation, turning almost completely white – apart from the black tip to its long, narrow tail.

It is from this that the Stoat gets its alternative winter name of Ermine, from the Old French word (via Middle English). The word 'ermine' also refers to the fur of the animal, which – with its distinctive black dots against a white background – was used from the medieval period onwards to line cloaks and coats, especially those of royalty and peers, and later judges. This custom lives on in the scientific name for the species, *Mustela erminea*.

Whereas the Mountain Hare and Ptarmigan moult into a white winter garb to avoid being caught and eaten, the Stoat turns white for a very different purpose. The camouflage enables this feisty little predator to conceal itself as it hunts. Despite its small size and weight – just ½ kg (1 lb) – the Stoat is able to kill a Mountain Hare up to eight times its own weight. This is due to its great speed, ability to twist and turn in pursuit of prey, and a set of very sharp teeth that makes short work of despatching an unfortunate hare with a quick and efficient bite to the neck.

Significant Highlanders

DAVID SEXTON ⋯ EAGLE RANGER

Born and brought up in London, David's childhood surroundings could hardly have been more different from where he lives and works today: the Isle of Mull. He first came here on a school field trip in the late 1970s, when his lifelong affair with the island began. After university in the USA, David began work with the RSPB. He soon returned to Mull to guard the first pair of reintroduced White-tailed Eagles to successfully raise a chick here. Having risen through the ranks of RSPB Scotland, in 2003 he decided to return to the field, and moved to Mull with his wife and two young daughters. He's never looked back.

Although David knows as well as anyone that the Highlands are not an unspoilt wilderness, he regards this as the closest in Britain to truly wild country, where you can get away from it all. The lack of crowds (and midges) is why he prefers autumn to any other season. The weather is often fine, with lovely autumnal colours and plenty of wildlife activity, from rutting Red Deer to Golden Eagles exploring new territories, while wild geese and swans arrive on the lochs.

Surprisingly, perhaps, for someone so closely associated with eagles, David's favourite Highland creature is the Pine Marten. He admires how it has made a comeback from persecution, and that it is so elusive and hard to see – making his first sighting, of an animal he hand-fed at a local B&B, even more special.

Although David lives and works on the Isle of Mull, his favourite Highland haunt is actually on the mainland – just about. The Ardnamurchan Peninsula is virtually an island, but boasts many of the mammals that some of the offshore islands lack. One of his favourite pastimes is looking out to sea on a summer's evening, and watching Minke Whales and Basking Sharks as the sun sets to the west.

Despite the many problems facing Highland wildlife, including the continued illegal shooting of raptors, David is optimistic about the future. He looks forward to species such as the Lynx making a comeback, and is passionate about communicating the wonders of Highland wildlife to the widest possible audience. Most of all, every time he sees a White-tailed Eagle soaring over his adoptive home, he can feel a great sense of pride as well as wonder at the return of this magnificent bird.

BIRDS LARGE AND SMALL

Two other creatures – one very large, one very small – share their high-mountain home with the Ptarmigan, Mountain Hare and Stoat. Both are birds: the huge and majestic Golden Eagle and the tiny Snow Bunting. A big female Golden Eagle can weigh more than 5 kg (11 lb), almost 150 times the weight of a Snow Bunting, which tips the scales at just 35 g (1¼ oz). Yet despite their vast differences in size and weight, they are both able to survive the winter here.

Snow Buntings probably manage to survive only with a helping hand from us. A flock usually hangs around the aptly named Ptarmigan Restaurant at the top of the funicular railway on Cairn Gorm, commuting back and forth to the car park lower down the mountain. Hikers, birders and skiers may take pity on the birds and give them a few crumbs to eat, and they also survive on food items dropped by visitors. When these are not available they peck at the snow to find tiny seeds of grasses and weeds. Nevertheless, given the meagre supply of food in winter and the difficulty finding it, it is likely that this flock is only able to stay here at this time of year (when most Snow Buntings have headed down to the coast) with help from human visitors.

These little birds are so tame that you may almost step on them before they take to the wing. When they do fly they reveal a flurry of white wings, flashing in the winter's air – hence their evocative Scottish folk names of snow flake, snow fowl and snow fleck. Yet although the Snow Bunting may appear small and delicate, it rivals the Ptarmigan for the title of the toughest bird in the world. Indeed, unlike the Ptarmigan, it has even been seen at the North Pole – the only one of the world's 5,000 or so songbird species ever to reach there.

They may differ vastly in size, but the massive Golden Eagle and the tiny Snow Bunting have both adapted to life in the harsh environment of the high tops.

Few birds are quite so magnificent and regal-looking as the Golden Eagle, one of the top predators of the Scottish Highlands.

Seeing Snow Buntings is pretty easy, at least in the middle of winter when they form flocks. The other species that lives here all year round, the Golden Eagle, may be much bigger, but despite its huge size it is much harder to see, for each pair has a massive territory over which the birds range far and wide.

The Golden Eagle is, paradoxically, one of the most familiar British birds, yet also one of the least familiar, for although everyone knows what it looks like, most people have never seen one. Even those who have caught sight of this magnificent bird have often had to make do with a distant view as it soars high in the sky, or disappears rapidly out of sight over a mountain ridge. It may be big, but the landscape where it lives is vast.

Our familiarity with the Golden Eagle is not one born of close encounters, but through its legendary qualities of power, strength and savagery. For these reasons it is an almost ubiquitous presence as an image of Scotland's wildlife and wild places, in books, TV programmes and even advertising.

It can sometimes be hard to distinguish myth from reality when it comes to iconic species, and this is especially true in the case of the Golden Eagle. We may

regard it as a ruthless hunter, yet Golden Eagles obtain much of their food by scavenging the carcasses of dead animals, especially during the long, harsh winter months. We may also think of it perched on a high mountain crag, yet many Golden Eagle nests (known as eyries) are actually sited halfway down a mountain, to avoid the birds wasting energy by carrying heavy prey upwards when they bring back food to the nest. Moreover, although we regard eagles to be magnificent, noble creatures, we may be shocked to discover that the elder of the two chicks often kills its younger sibling by taking the lion's share of the food brought back by its parents, so that the smaller bird eventually starves to death (see also p. 143).

Even when you do glimpse a large raptor soaring above a glen or mountain, you need to make sure of its true identity. Many visitors from the south have returned home from the Highlands convinced that they have seen a Golden Eagle, even though the bird they actually saw was a Common Buzzard – not for nothing are buzzards known in Scotland as 'tourist eagles'.

When you do catch sight of the real thing – even momentarily – there really should be no mistaking it. Golden Eagles are simply huge, with a wingspan of

2 m (well over 6 ft), long, broad wings with prominent 'fingers' made up of the outer primary feathers, and a large head and bill. They glide or soar effortlessly in the air, using thermal air currents to stay aloft, before folding the wings into the body and plummeting down towards the earth to catch their prey.

If you are lucky enough to get a closer look, the dark brown plumage, set off by golden patches on the sides of the neck and pale markings across the wings, is very distinctive. You may need to search for a long time. Golden Eagles don't spend much of their lives in flight – it is very costly in terms of energy – and often perch inconspicuously on a cliff face or crag, where their plumage blends in with the rocks.

During the short hours of daylight in the winter months the birds are often more active, quartering their huge territory in search of prey such as Mountain Hares, Ptarmigan and Red Grouse. Alternatively they may be looking out for a dead sheep or deer, which will provide a welcome meal – carrion makes up the majority of the winter diet of most Scottish Golden Eagles.

Feeding regularly is essential if the birds are to get enough energy to survive, yet feeding isn't their only concern at this time of year. Golden Eagles return to the area where they nest well before the New Year, usually coming back to a long-established eyrie, which may have seen several generations of birds nesting here over many decades.

By January they have refurbished and repaired their nest (which may have been damaged by autumn gales), following which the pair sometimes engage in a spectacular display flight, each bird swooping high into the sky before plunging down and up again like a rollercoaster. This helps strengthen the existing pair bond before the serious process of nesting begins again.

Later in the year these two mammal and three bird species breed on the high tops. They are joined by a handful of other species adapted to do so in what is still a very harsh environment, even in spring and summer. But for now they have the place to themselves – and apart from a handful of hardy human visitors, will do so until the snows begin to melt and spring finally arrives at the very top of this Highland world.

It may look like a fierce hunter but, in winter especially, much of the Golden Eagle's food is obtained by scavenging.

SPRING STIRS IN THE FORESTS

February may be the height of winter on the high tops of the Cairngorm plateau, but in the wooded valleys down below the mountains something is definitely stirring. At the very top of a tall, stately Scots Pine, a bird is calling to its mate with a series of hard, almost metallic sounds: 'chup, chup, chup'. A pair of Scottish Crossbills is settling down to breed.

A Scots Pine seedling – one of the three native conifer species in Britain, the others being the juniper and the yew.

The male is brick-red in colour, with darker wings and tail. His mate is a drabber shade of moss-green, enabling her to stay camouflaged when incubating her precious eggs. Apart from the Hawfinch, crossbills are the largest members of the finch family in Britain, noticeably bigger and bulkier than a Chaffinch, with thick necks and a large head.

Crossbills are unique among birds. The four or more species (depending on whose taxonomy you follow) are the only ones of the world's 10,000 or more bird species to have this unique bill shape, with the upper mandible crossing over the lower one in what looks remarkably like a pair of pincers. That, in essence, is exactly what the bills are: a crossbill uses its specially shaped bill to tease out the tiny seeds of pine cones in order to feed on them. Because no other birds can do this, crossbills have a huge advantage over the birds with which they share their forest habitat. It enables them to breed at a time when their fellow finches and tits are simply trying to find enough food to survive the winter. Thus from early February, a pair of Scottish Crossbills will begin to make a nest, usually in a sunnier part of the forest where the birds can take advantage of added warmth from the weak winter sunlight.

Despite its limited range, the Scottish Crossbill is fairly catholic in its choice of habitat. As well as breeding in Scots Pines, it will also nest in Sitka Spruces, Larches and Lodgepole Pines – all foreign tree species introduced into Scotland, and mainly grown in plantations for timber.

The nest is a bulky, cup-shaped structure made from conifer twigs, moss, grass and heather, and lined with hair or feathers, constructed mainly by the female with some help from her mate. It is usually situated on a horizontal branch near the very top of the tree – perhaps 20 m (65 ft) or more above the ground. The female lays three or four eggs, which hatch after just 12–14 days, so there is often snow on the ground and night-time temperatures are well below freezing when the tiny chicks are in the nest.

Because the crossbills have a reliable supply of food in the form of the papery seeds of pine cones, the young are able to thrive, and they usually fledge and leave the nest three weeks after hatching. However, the parents keep feeding them for another eight weeks or so to ensure that they survive in the harsh, cold climate. Nevertheless, their lives are brief: the longest surviving ringed bird died at less than three years old.

The once impressive Caledonian Forest covers only a tiny fraction of its original range across much of Scotland.

Endemic species

The Scottish Crossbill is the only bird species endemic to the British Isles, found nowhere else in the world. Once that accolade went to the Red Grouse, but scientists have since discovered that the British Red Grouse is genetically very close to its much more widespread cousin the Willow Grouse (also known as the Willow Ptarmigan), even though the two look very different.

As well as the smaller-billed Common Crossbill, which is also found widely throughout the rest of Britain, and the huge-billed Parrot Crossbill (once only a rare and occasional visitor to Britain, but now established as a scarce breeding bird, also in the Highlands), there was a third group of birds with bills in between the size of the Common and Parrot Crossbills. After they were studied in detail, including careful analysis of differences in their bill measurements and testing of their DNA, it was finally decided that these belonged to a new and uniquely British species: the Scottish Crossbill.

Today, it is thought that there are about 7,000 Scottish Crossbills, confined to the north-east Highlands of Scotland, with strongholds in Strathspey and Deeside, and smaller populations from Inverness-shire north to Sutherland. The true picture is undoubtedly confused by two factors: first, the difficulty of firmly identifying Scottish Crossbills in the field, especially separating them from the very similar Parrot Crossbill; and second, the nomadic habits of all crossbill species, due to which these pine forests may be invaded by large flocks of Common Crossbills from time to time.

WINTER FLOCKS

Meanwhile, elsewhere in the forest, most small birds are simply concentrating on surviving at a time of year when the daytime temperature may not rise above freezing, while at night the mercury can plummet to 10 or even 20 degrees below zero. They do so by forming flocks: many pairs of eyes make finding food easier, and also help them avoid being caught and eaten by Sparrowhawks and other predators like feral cats, of which there are an estimated 100,000 on the loose in the Highlands.

The most common and most showy small bird in winter – and indeed at most other times of year – is the Chaffinch. If this were a rare visitor to our shores, the Chaffinch would be regarded as a great beauty, but because it is common, familiar and widespread throughout Britain, its charms are often ignored.

The male Chaffinch is a truly handsome little bird about the size of a sparrow and similar in shape, but with a much more distinctive plumage. The grey crown and nape contrast with a chestnut back, dark wings with two white wing-bars, and a deep rose-pink face, chest and belly. When he takes to the wing the white wing-bars flash in the sunlight, and he also reveals a moss-green rump as he flies away. His mate, by contrast, is far drabber, although she sports a similar basic pattern. She superficially resembles a female House Sparrow, but is neater and cleaner looking, with brown above and below, and those clear white wing-bars.

In the Scottish Highlands the Chaffinch is often the first bird you see as you get out of your car. It gathers in large flocks in car parks, picking up natural food but also taking advantage of our wasteful habits by taking any food we deliberately or inadvertently leave behind.

Few British songbirds are quite as colourful and attractive as a male Chaffinch a common and familiar bird throughout the Highlands.

Siskin (top) and Brambling (bottom) can be seen in good numbers in the woods and forests of the Highlands in winter. Both often visit bird tables and feeders in search of energy-giving food.

At this time of year it's worth checking Chaffinch flocks carefully, for they may also contain the Chaffinch's close relative, the Brambling. These birds stand out by virtue of their more orange plumage, darker head (in the case of the male) and especially their white rump as they take to the wing.

The Brambling is the northern European equivalent of the Chaffinch, and although a handful of pairs occasionally breed in Scotland, it is primarily an autumn and winter visitor to Britain. In some years millions fly across the North Sea to spend the winter here, and in others far fewer appear – perhaps only a few tens of thousands. This depends on the state of the beech-mast crop, their favourite food.

If you want to see the other small birds in these dense, forbidding forests, one good tip is to find a birdfeeder, such as those at the RSPB reserve at Loch Garten in Speyside. These attract Chaffinches and Bramblings, which often feed on spilt seed beneath the feeders, as well as a range of other finch and tit species.

In southern Britain a flash of green and yellow is most likely to come from a Greenfinch. Here, a closer look reveals a smaller bird, with dark streaks among the green of its plumage: a Siskin. Sociable little birds, their

stronghold used to be the northern coniferous forests, but they have now extended their breeding range southwards into southern England and Wales. They are still common here, however, their numbers boosted in winter by immigrants from further north and east.

Siskins use their needle-sharp bills to extract seeds from conifers, but like most small birds will always take advantage of an easy supply of food in the form of seeds or peanuts provided by us. As they fly on and off feeders their wings flash with yellow patches, brighter in the male.

Like any seed feeders anywhere in the country, the feeders here attract members of the tit family. Blue, Great and Coal Tits all sport their own variation on the same basic pattern. All have white cheeks, while the Great Tit has a black head, green back, bluish wings and canary-yellow underparts bisected with a black stripe (wider in the male than in the female). The Blue Tit is also yellow underneath with green back and bluish wings, but has a bright blue cap and lacks the black stripe down the front of its larger relative.

The Coal Tit – the shyest of the three species – is a monochrome version of its cousins. With a black cap, white cheeks, brown back and brownish wash to its pale underparts, it also sports a very distinctive white patch on the back of its neck, making it fairly easy to identify.

The real prize here is a much rarer member of the tit family, confined to the Scottish Highlands and mainly found in pine forests between Strathspey and the Moray Firth, north and south of the Great Glen. This is the Crested Tit. Superficially similar to the more common Coal Tit, but with a plainer brown back, greyish-brown underparts and the distinctive wispy crest that gives the species its name, the Crested Tit is a hard bird to see, even here in its Highland stronghold.

Crested Tits often feed high in the forest canopy, hanging acrobatically beneath the branches and twigs to search for tiny insects, where you may find them by listening for their distinctive trilling sounds. They also visit seed and nut feeders, such as those at Loch Garten, where they are used to visitors and allow close and prolonged views. In winter Crested Tits often join forces with other small birds such as Great, Blue and Coal Tits, Treecreepers and Goldcrests, keeping in touch with one another by the constant uttering of tiny, high-pitched contact calls.

Given that the Crested Tit is widespread on mainland Europe, it's a bit of a puzzle why its range is so restricted in Britain. Despite plenty of seemingly ideal habitats Crested Tits haven't even reached the forests of Deeside, just a stone's throw east of their current range.

It appears that the distinctive Scottish race descends from a population isolated from the rest of Europe's Crested Tits sometime during the last ice age. It developed a preference for the specific forest habitat found here: tall pine trees with an understorey of heather that attracts the insects on which the birds feed in spring and summer, and standing dead trees in which they usually nest. The population, estimated at 1,000–2,000 pairs, is mainly sedentary – which may also explain why the birds are confined to this small area of the Highlands.

Crested Tits are, like their commoner relatives, endlessly active and very curious, often giving superb close-up views.

RED REFUGE

Crested Tits and Scottish Crossbills can sometimes be hard to see, but compared with the mammals that inhabit these vast Highland forests they are far from tricky. There are species here that are also found throughout Britain, such as the Red Fox, Badger, Stoat and Weasel. But there are also three other far more rare and elusive creatures: the Red Squirrel, Pine Marten and Scottish Wildcat.

Apart from the tiny tweets of birds hanging in the cold February air, these forests can seem almost devoid of life at this time of year. But as you walk along the paths, a telltale rustling in the branches of a snow-covered pine suggests that at least one creature is stirring. Moments later, another movement, as more and more snow falls off the branch and down onto the ground below. Then a head appears, followed by a sleek, sinuous body and a long, bushy tail. The head turns to reveal two vertical tufts, beady black eyes and a quizzical expression. A Red Squirrel is looking down at you from its arboreal perch.

This is our only native species of squirrel, and one of only two species native to Europe (the other, the Persian Squirrel, is confined to Turkey in the extreme south-east of the continent). By contrast, the Red Squirrel is common and widespread across much of Europe, from Spain and Portugal in the south and west, to Scandinavia and Russia in the north and east. Indeed, it is a familiar creature in many European cities as well as the wider countryside. It would, of course, be far more common and widespread in Britain, were it not for the deliberate and misguided introduction of the alien North American Grey Squirrel during the second half of the 19th century. From

After being pushed northwards by the invading Grey Squirrel, the Red Squirrel's stronghold is now the Scottish Highlands.

Red squirrels are, like all members of their family, fantastically agile, especially when running along narrow branches up in the forest canopy.

just a couple of pairs released on a Cheshire country estate, there are now as many as 3 million Grey Squirrels at large in Britain, in most of England, Wales and Northern Ireland, and across the central belt of lowland Scotland.

Unfortunately, Grey Squirrels both outcompete their red cousins and carry a disease that, although harmless to the Greys, rapidly kills the Reds. Because of this, Red Squirrels are now mostly confined on mainland Britain to Northumberland and the Lake District in England, and the Highlands of Scotland, where roughly three-quarters of the entire UK population (120,000 of about 160,000 individuals) now lives. Fortunately – so far at least – the Greys have not managed to invade the dense Highland forests. Given the determination of conservationists to stop them from doing so, by organised culling if necessary, for the moment at least the Scottish Red Squirrels appear to be safe.

Red Squirrels are highly arboreal animals, spending the majority of their lives clambering acrobatically around the trees, although they do also feed down on the ground from time to time. That bushy tail isn't just there for decoration: it helps the animal keep its

balance, especially when it is leaping from branch to branch, many metres above the ground.

Unlike some mammals Red Squirrels are unable to store large amounts of fat in their bodies, so they need to feed almost constantly when awake. In winter this means that they have to be constantly active, spending as much as 80 per cent of the short hours of daylight looking for, finding and eating food. They use their front paws to hold and manipulate nuts and seeds, making feeding more efficient.

They also have a trick up their sleeve to cope with bad weather. During the autumn, when food is more plentiful, they store pine cones beneath the surface of the soil. In the harsh winter months they use their excellent spatial memory to find them and dig them up – an easy meal at a tough time of year.

Red Squirrels don't just feed in the forest canopy – eating mainly pine cones, seeds and occasionally berries, bark and lichens – but sleep and nest there, too. Their nests – known as dreys – are large, rounded objects made from twigs, leaves and moss, which they use as both a night-time dormitory and a place to raise a family in spring.

ACROBAT OF THE PINES

Red Squirrels don't have all that many enemies, especially in the Highlands. However, one agile member of the Stoat and Weasel family does occasionally manage to catch one. The Pine Marten is one of our most scarce and beautiful mammals. Once found across a wide range of Britain's woods and forests, by the turn of the 19th century it had already disappeared from much of lowland Britain. Today it is virtually confined to Scotland and a few parts of Northern Ireland, although there are now plans to reintroduce it into parts of England and Wales. One reason to do this is because it preys on the Grey Squirrel, and might thus help protect the native Reds and allow them to re-establish themselves in some of their former haunts.

The reason, incidentally, why Red Squirrels can coexist here with Pine Martens is that the squirrels are very light, weighing only about 250–300 g (9–10 oz). They are thus able to seek refuge at the ends of branches, which the much heavier Pine Martens (weighing 1.3–2.2 kg/3–5 lb) cannot usually reach. The heavier Grey Squirrels are unable to do this, so often fall victim to the marten's powerful jaws.

When up in the trees Pine Martens are amazingly agile. They are able to leap as much as 4 m (13 ft) from branch to branch, or drop more than 20 m (65 ft) to the ground. Seen well – and you don't often get the chance for prolonged views – a Pine Marten is a very handsome beast indeed. The lustrous chestnut-brown fur on the face, head, body and tail is set off by a creamy-yellow patch that extends from the throat to the belly. The animals are long and slender – like a giant Stoat in size and shape – reaching an overall length, including the long tail, of up to 80 cm (30 in).

Closely related to the Polecat, Stoat and Weasel, the Pine Marten is one of our rarest and most elusive mammals.

Pine Martens are opportunistic feeders, feeding on a wide range of food from rodents to peanut butter sandwiches!

Like many forest-dwelling mammals Pine Martens are mainly nocturnal, spending the day resting up on a branch in a tree, before heading out to feed as dusk falls. In winter in these dense forests, this may be as early as 3 o'clock in the afternoon. They usually come down to the ground to hunt, searching for small mammals such as mice, voles and Rabbits, but also eating small birds if they can catch them, and foraging on berries in the autumn.

In recent years Pine Martens have also learnt – like Red Squirrels – that food can be had for free. They come to bird tables even during the daytime, feasting on jam sandwiches (they have a particularly sweet tooth) or, in more refined settings, on peanut butter. At the Aigas Field Centre, near Beauly, west of Inverness, Pine Martens come regular as clockwork every night to feed in front of a hide installed specially to give visitors the chance to get a really close view of these magnificent animals. Watching one at such close quarters as it shins up and down to reach its free meal is a great privilege, and gives you a real insight into its behaviour.

The good news about Pine Martens is that although numbers are still much lower than they once were (there are now 3,000–4,000 individuals in the wild), they are on the increase, as nowadays persecution is much less of a problem than it used to be. As a result they are increasingly being seen away from their Highland stronghold, even on the edge of cities such as Glasgow and Edinburgh. Nevertheless, they remain one of our rarest native mammals.

EVELYN SPENCE ⋯ KILTMAKER AND BEEKEEPER

Having been born and brought up in a croft on the west coast of Scotland, Evelyn was surrounded by farm animals from an early age. Her earliest memories are of going with her father to fetch the plough horse they used to borrow from a neighbour, and collecting the cows from the fields for milking.

Evelyn recalls that she was forever arriving home with some creature she had come across during her daily routine. During haymaking she was most interested in finding the Field Mice and relocating them to pastures new. Some little orphaned mice would often be evicted from her pockets in the evenings over dinner.

The second in a family of five, Evelyn left school at 18 to begin a five-year apprenticeship in kiltmaking in Inverness. After a short gap while she raised her two daughters, she and her husband moved to a smallholding in Farr, south of Inverness, where she began her thriving business.

She became a beekeeper by a happy accident, when two hives brought to her property were abandoned and she found hundreds of dead bees on the ground. Opening a hive, she was mesmerised by the sight – and was hooked. Today she breeds queen bees, choosing characteristics that will help them survive the worst of the Highland weather.

Evelyn loves the beauty of the Highlands and its diversity of wildlife. Her favourite season is autumn, with its changing colours, but from the wildlife's point of view it has to be the spring, with all the new life that begins then.

Two years ago Evelyn put her childhood expertise in raising orphaned animals to the test on a bigger scale, when a baby Roe Deer lived with her family in their house. She was continually amazed by the animal's intelligence. It rapidly became housetrained, knocking on the door when it wanted to come in and be fed, then sitting comfortably by the fire to watch television! Later the deer returned to the wild, but she still returns regularly to see them.

Evelyn does worry about the Highlands' future, especially as we seem so obsessed with material progress, wanting bigger, better and cheaper, which puts wildlife a poor second. She thinks people are now so busy that they forget to take time out, and advises us to stop, shut our eyes and listen to the wonderful array of natural sounds around us.

THE HIGHLAND TIGER

Pine Martens are not, thankfully, as rare as the other specialist carnivore of these Caledonian pine forests – the Scottish Wildcat, which may now be down to as few as 50 pure-bred individuals.

Technically this species is part of a much larger population of wild cats, *Felis silvestris*, whose vast range extends all the way across the northern parts of Europe and Asia, making it the largest of any cat species. However, given that the unique Scottish race, *grampia*, has been separated from its mainland Eurasian relatives for well over 100,000 years, it is very definitely worth saving. It is also – in the absence of the Eurasian Lynx, Grey Wolf and Brown Bear, all of which used to roam these forests – the only fierce predator we have.

Sadly, however, we may not have the Scottish Wildcat for much longer. Once threatened by persecution and habitat loss, which drove it back from its original range across much of Britain to its final stronghold in the Scottish Highlands, the Scottish Wildcat is now under threat from a much greater problem. The presence of up to 100,000 feral cats at large in the Highlands has led to widespread interbreeding between wild and domestic animals, and this has so diluted the gene pool that virtually every 'Scottish Wildcat' carries at least some domesticated cat genes. This is not always obvious in the field, especially as this elusive, largely nocturnal animal rarely gives prolonged views.

Our rarest and most elusive mammal, the Scottish Wildcat, has been driven to the edge of extinction over the past century, thanks to the spread of feral cats, with which it interbreeds.

True wildcats are often hard to tell apart from hybrids. Look for the distinctive tail pattern and bushy tails.

Several schemes are now trying to save the Scottish Wildcat from what appears to be imminent oblivion. Some advocate captive breeding and eventual release of the kittens into the wild, although this does require careful genetic testing of any breeding stock to make sure that it is pure-bred (or as pure-bred as possible). Others believe that the only way to save the Scottish Wildcat is to put any remaining pure-bred animals into secluded areas, then catch and neuter any feral cats in the area so that the two cannot interbreed.

If you are lucky enough to come across any 'wildcat' in the Highlands, it is crucial to check the key identification features of a truly wild animal. It should be very large – up to 1 m (39 in) long – and show a distinctive bushy tail with a blunt tip and thick black rings around it. However, even experts sometimes struggle to tell wild and feral animals apart.

Wild cats used to be far more widespread across Britain and Ireland, found in woodland and hilly habitats throughout England and Wales as well as in Scotland. Sometime around the late Bronze Age or Iron Age (approximately 2,000 years ago) they went extinct in Ireland, but they could still be found in southern Britain until the sixteenth century, until habitat loss and hunting from a growing human population meant they could no longer survive. They managed to cling on in the wilder upland regions of northern England Wales until the 1880s, by which time persecution – helped by the invention of the breech-loading shotgun – led to their disappearance there too.

The Caledonian pine forests

The vast expanses of pine forest that blanket the hills and valleys below the Cairngorm plateau may look impressive, but in fact they are but a tiny fraction – a little over 1 per cent – of the forests that were once here.

The Caledonian Forest got its name from the Roman writer Pliny the Elder, who lived in the 1st century AD and perished in the eruption of Mt Vesuvius at Pompeii. He wrote of the 'silva Caledonia' – or 'wood of Caledonia' (the Latin name for what is now Scotland). But the Caledonian pine forests themselves are far older than this, having begun to colonise the Highlands after the end of the last ice age, in about 7000 BC. For a while they flourished in the cool, dry climate, but as the climate began to warm up, in around 5000 BC, the area covered by Scots Pines began to shrink.

As human civilisation grew and the population of the Highlands also began to rise, so these mighty trees were chopped down for timber and fuel, and to provide land for grazing sheep. Today the forest, which once extended over more than 15,000 sq km (60,000 sq miles) now covers a mere 180 sq km (70 sq miles). The habitat has also been fragmented, so that the blanket of pines that once stretched almost from coast to coast is now no more.

Fortunately, these forests remain ecologically special, not least due to an unbroken run of 9,000 years of isolation from other wooded habitats. This explains why they still hold wild creatures either not found anywhere else in the UK, or whose populations here are by far the most crucial in terms of the British fauna. These include the Scottish Wildcat, Pine Marten, Red Squirrel, Capercaillie, Black Grouse, Crested Tit, and Parrot and Scottish Crossbills.

COURTSHIP ON THE WATER

The mountains and forests are just two of the main habitats for wildlife in the Highlands, but there are three other habitats that, although very different, share one thing in common, namely water.

The lochs and rivers of the Highlands – ranging from narrow streams to raging rivers, and tiny lochans to vast lochs – are incredibly important for both the creatures that take advantage of them to drink and bathe, and those that spend the whole (or at least a crucial part) of their lives here. On the edge of the region, the coasts and seas to the west and east are also crucial refuges for both visiting and resident wildlife.

As February gives way to March, and the days gradually become lighter as the northern hemisphere turns back towards the sun and the spring equinox approaches, so the thoughts of many wild creatures turn to love – or to put it more accurately, to breeding and reproduction.

For many species, especially the birds of the region, the next few months are crucial. If they fail in the race to reproduce – and many do, through predation, bad weather or simply bad luck – they may never get the chance to do so again. If this happens their genetic heritage is lost forever. If they succeed, however, their offspring will continue their line down the generations. Breeding starts, for most species, with courtship, and often the best place to see courtship displays in the Highlands is on the water.

Divers rival grebes as the most aquatic of all the world's birds. They rarely emerge from the water onto land, doing so only when breeding and even then struggling to move on land at all. This is because their legs are positioned very far back on the body to enable them to swim and dive most effectively.

One of our most handsome and striking waterbirds, the Slavonian Grebe is confined as a British breeding bird to the Scottish Highlands. These birds are beginning their spring courtship displays, and are in full breeding plumage.

The male Eider is Britain's largest and one of our most handsome ducks – this bird is displaying to a watching female.

OVERLEAF Whooper Swans are one of our largest and heaviest birds. Flocks arrive in the Highlands each autumn from their breeding grounds in Iceland.

Three species of diver – Red-throated, Black-throated and Great Northern – spend the winter in and around the Scottish Highlands, mostly offshore. A fourth, the White-billed Diver, is a rare passage migrant along the coasts in April and May, as it heads back north to its Arctic breeding grounds. Despite the children's story *Great Northern*, written by Arthur Ransome, our largest diver has never been proven to breed in Britain, but the two smaller species, the Red-throated and Black-throated, do. Both usually nest on remote lochs in the less populous areas of the Highlands, so to see breeding divers you usually need to travel to the more far-flung parts of the region, such as Wester Ross, Caithness and Sutherland.

In North America divers are known as loons, perhaps because they are considered stupid birds, but more likely the word is a representation of their haunting calls. When courting, divers often utter these strange and beguiling sounds, which carry long distances in the otherwise silent late-winter landscape.

Meanwhile, on the coasts to the west and east of the Highlands, other birds are pairing up, too. Whooper Swans are strengthening their bonds before they fly back across the sea to Iceland. Pink-footed Geese have even further to travel: from the RSPB reserve at the Loch of Strathbeg between Fraserburgh and Peterhead, perhaps as far as Greenland.

Offshore, rafts of seaducks float on the sea, bobbing up and down like a flotilla of rubber ducks in a particularly turbulent bath. Most are scoters – of the Common and Velvet variety, both of which are almost entirely dark apart from a splash of custard-yellow on their bills – but there are also large rafts of Common Eiders, the brown females being wooed by the black-and-white males. These may look rather butch, but they have the least masculine call of any British bird, sounding like a cross between an indignant maiden aunt and the late Frankie Howerd. Soon they will pair off and breed along the same coasts where they spend the winter; surprisingly perhaps, they are our second most common breeding duck after the ubiquitous Mallard. Meanwhile the scoters will mostly head north to Scandinavia and Arctic Russia, although a handful of pairs of Common Scoters do breed in the Flow Country in the north of the Highlands – perhaps 50 nesting pairs in most years.

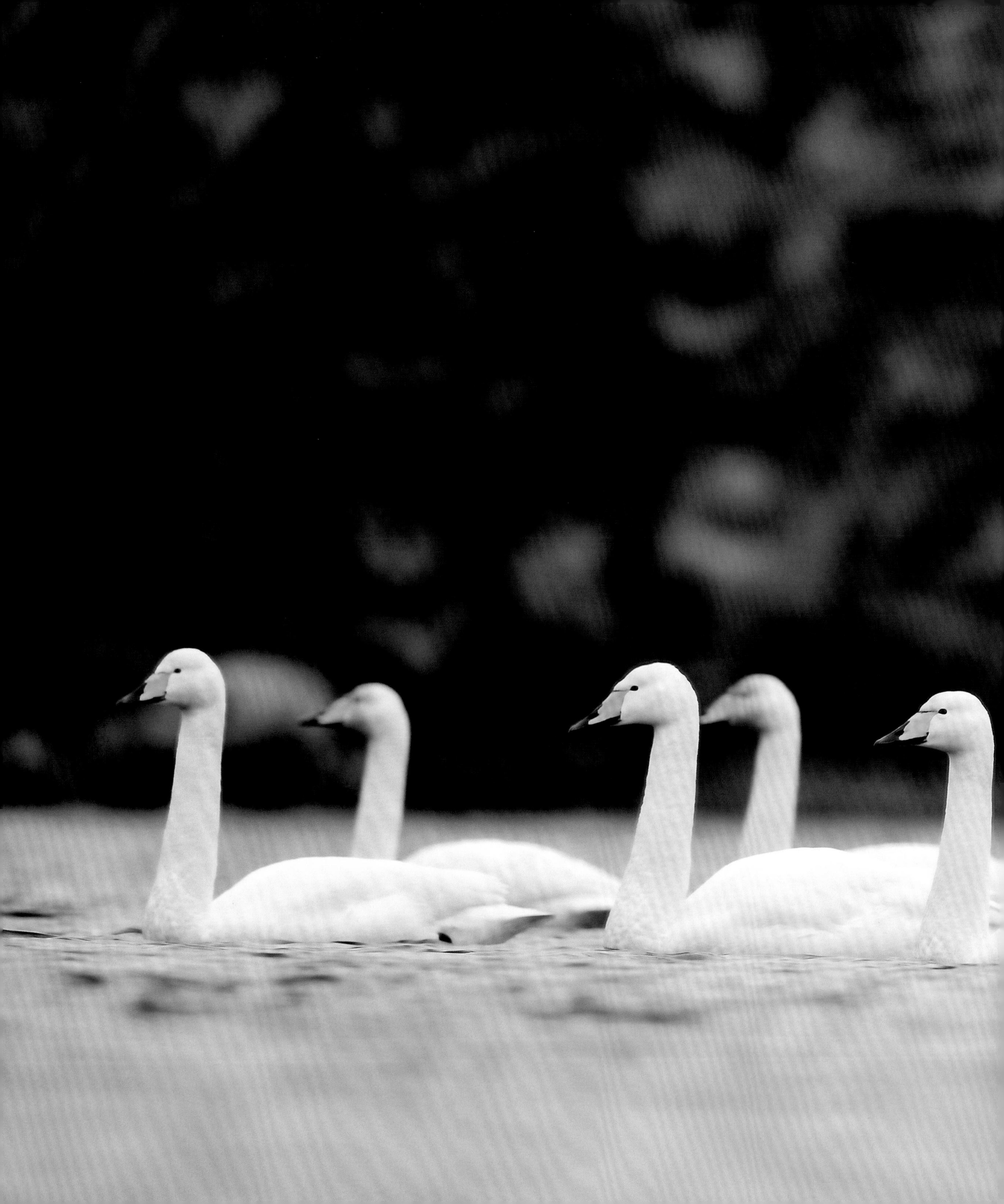

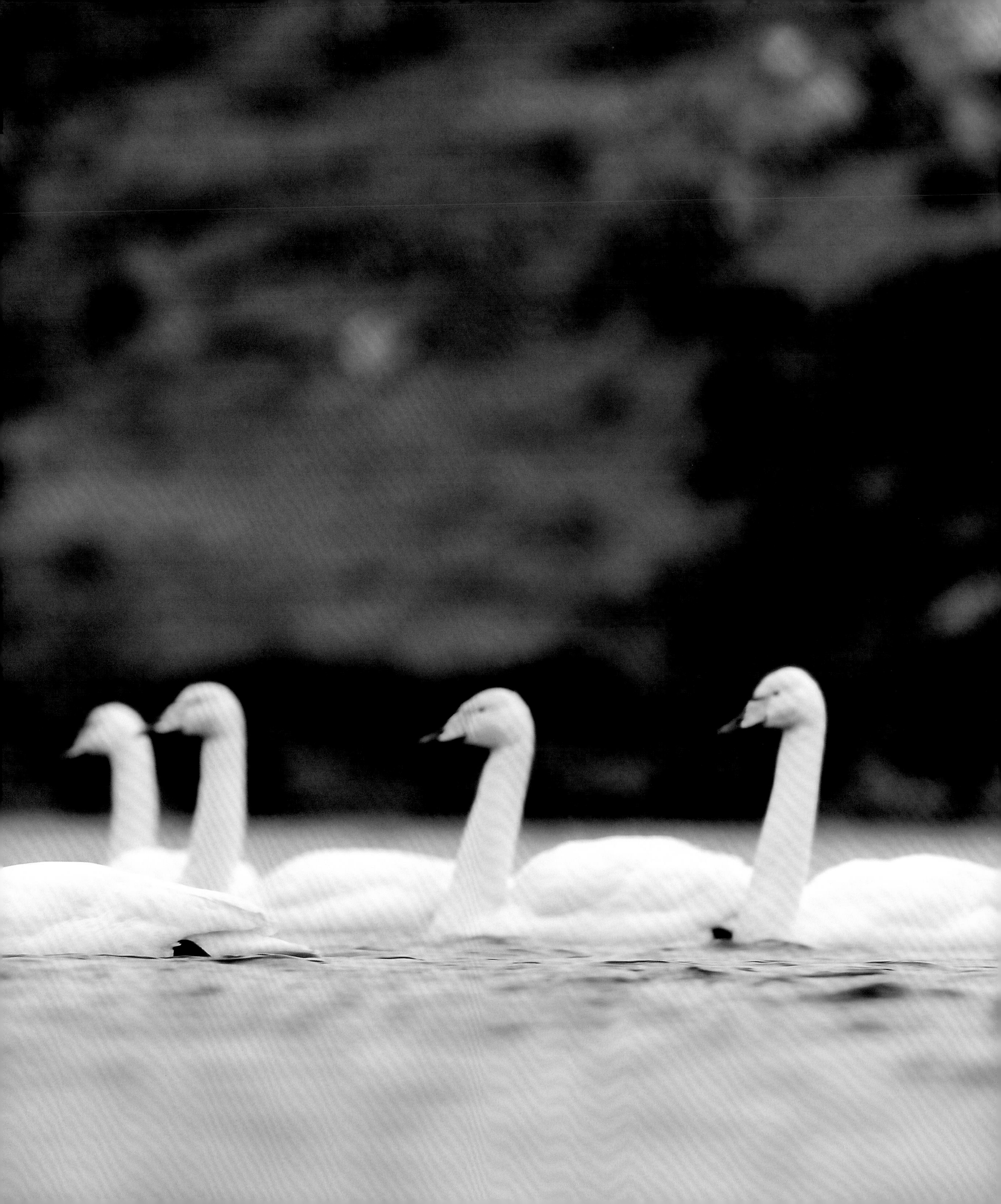

MISSING – EXPECTED SOON?

This whistle-stop tour of the Scottish Highlands in the depths of winter sets the scene not just for what is happening now, but for what is to come. The birds and mammals braving the harsh winter cold of the mountains, moors, lochs, forests and coasts are already either thinking about breeding or have already begun. It may still be chilly, but as the days lengthen the promise of spring is – however hard it may be to imagine – just around the corner.

What of the creatures we haven't seen – or at least, not so far? What about those that are absent or missing in winter, either because they have travelled far away to avoid the cold and find food, or simply because they are dormant, hidden or hibernating until the warm weather finally arrives?

Some have gone a long way indeed. The most spectacular journey is that made by the 30 or so species of bird that return from Africa to breed here in the Highlands, to take advantage of the long spring and summer days, and plentiful supplies of food. These include warblers, flycatchers and chats, larger birds such as the Cuckoo and Hobby, waders such as the Dotterel, Wood and Green Sandpipers, and birds of prey including the famous Osprey and the more elusive Honey-buzzard.

Common Sandpipers are just one of several species of bird that travel all the way from Africa to breed in the Scottish Highlands.

Puffins will soon be returning to their breeding colonies on isolated headlands and offshore islands, having spent the entire winter out at sea.

Many of Scotland's seabirds – shearwaters and skuas, terns and auks – have also been a long way away, either off the coasts of Africa or somewhere in the North Atlantic. They too will soon return and get down to the urgent business of raising a family on offshore islands off the north-west coast of Sutherland.

It is almost impossible to imagine how different the lives of these birds are at present: Swallows hawking for insects between herds of African Elephant and Wildebeest; Puffins bobbing up and down on the surface of the water hundreds of miles from land; Cuckoos hiding in the African rainforest; or a Common Sandpiper feeding at the edge of a waterhole, carefully avoiding the local crocodiles. They will soon return to a very different life here.

They are just a few of the creatures that will soon appear. Butterflies and moths are nowhere to be seen, yet they are still here, either hibernating or in their pupae, waiting to hatch out as soon as it is warm enough in April or May. Dragonflies and damselflies – including several species confined in Britain to the Highlands – are here too, this time hidden underwater in the form of predatory nymphs.

Hedgehogs are hibernating, while many other mammals such as voles and shrews are lying low. In the depths of Loch Ness, something is stirring: huge fish known as ferox trout (from the Latin meaning 'wild') are emerging from the dark waters to pair up and spawn. Way out in the Atlantic, a salmon is starting its epic journey back to the place where it was born – a journey that won't be completed until the autumn.

Meanwhile, as the spring equinox passes and for the first time for six months, the days are longer than the nights. Life begins to move apace, here in the Scottish Highlands.

Spring into Summer

THE HIGHLAND CHORUS

Birdsong comes late to the Highlands. Down south, in the gardens of the Home Counties, Wrens are trilling for most of the winter, Great Tits are singing their seesaw serenade from early January, and even Song Thrushes may begin their repetitive, measured tune soon after New Year.

Here in the Caledonian pine forests that line the Spey Valley and Deeside, things are very different. Amid great swathes of dark green foliage, impenetrable to sunlight and dusted with snow, the resident birds have been far too busy trying to stay alive to bother to defend a territory or attract a mate.

It's been a long, hard winter, and many small birds have only managed to survive due to the kindness of people. For the past few months the residents of Banchory and Boat of Garten, Nethy Bridge and Nairn, Braemar and Beauly have been putting out nuts, seeds and balls of fat on their bird tables and in their hanging feeders, providing just enough for the birds to get the energy they need to survive the long, cold winter nights.

Now, however, the Blackbirds, Song Thrushes, Greenfinches and Goldfinches have mostly left their temporary winter refuges and returned to the forest. As the spring equinox tips the balance in favour of warmth and light in the Highlands, and indeed all the way across the northern hemisphere, they are starting to think about the breeding season.

The Caledonian pine forests fall silent in winter, when many birds move away. Come the spring birdsong echoes around the Scots Pines once again, as woodland species return to breed.

Two of the classic birds of the Caledonian pine forests – the Coal Tit (top) and Goldcrest (bottom) – both of which are best located by listening for their high-pitched calls or penetrating, rhythmic songs.

The next three months – from the spring equinox, towards the end of March, through to Midsummer's Day in late June, are make or break time for these small birds – as indeed they are for all the birdlife, most of the plants and the majority of the mammals that make their homes in the Scottish Highlands. For the wild creatures that live here are about to enjoy a bonanza of food, fuelled by the long days of spring and summer. Plenty of food gives them the chance to do what their whole lives have been leading up to so far – to reproduce.

If they succeed they pass on their genes to the next generation, but if they fail they may never do so. Most of these small birds rarely make it past their second birthday, so this coming breeding season is absolutely crucial. This is why, well before dawn on a frosty morning towards the end of March, the forest canopy resounds with birdsong.

There is the rhythmic, high-pitched sound of the Coal Tit, accompanied by the even higher pitched (and equally syncopated) song of the tiny Goldcrest. Treecreepers sing their buzzy notes from deep inside the pine foliage, while a pair of Crested Tits – found here and nowhere else in Britain (see p. 44) – investigates a hole in a dead birch tree, where in a week or so they will begin to make their nest.

Many birds are still to arrive. The Willow Warblers, Chiffchaffs and Blackcaps are way to the south, somewhere in Africa or around the shores of the Mediterranean, on their way back home. The Osprey, the most famous bird of these lochs and forests, is coming back, too. Tracking devices reveal that some birds have now crossed the Straits of Gibraltar and will soon arrive here.

For now, the resident species hold sway – the tough guys who stayed put during the winter rather than seeking warmer climes – and it is their sound that wakes the forest each morning in the Highland Chorus.

GOLDEN WONDER

In any poll of Britain's most beautiful waterbirds, the Slavonian Grebe would stand a pretty good chance of winning. Intermediate in size between our largest (Great Crested) and smallest (Little) Grebes, the Slavonian is a little larger, and more sleek and slender, than the very similar Black-necked Grebe.

In winter Slavonian Grebes look rather like Guillemots or Razorbills. They are basically black and white, with grey shading on the neck and flanks, and a bright red eye. However, when they moult into their breeding plumage in late March or early April, they are transformed. The monochrome shades are replaced by a deep chestnut neck and body, darker grey wings and a black head – all set off with a tuft of rich golden-yellow feathers above and behind the eye. It is this plumage feature that gave the species its North American name of Horned Grebe (the name Slavonian, incidentally, comes either from the northern Russian region of Sclavonia or, as some believe, the Croatian region of Slavonia).

Slavonian Grebes are a very rare breeding bird in Britain, and their stronghold is the small lochs and lochans of the Scottish Highlands. The species first bred here (and indeed anywhere in Britain) in the opening decade of the 20th century, and has struggled to maintain its foothold ever since. In the 1970s numbers peaked at around 80 pairs, but today there are probably fewer than 20 pairs, at least half of them at a single site, Loch Ruthven, an RSPB reserve a few miles south of Inverness. Sadly, even those that do breed struggle to raise their young. Although grebes are excellent parents, carrying their tiny chicks on their backs to keep them safe, the youngsters often fall victim to Pike or other predators.

As in other grebes, the display is a truly ornate affair. One bird dives beneath the surface of the loch, then emerges next to its mate; the birds then rise up in the water and dance alongside one another like a couple doing a tango. This helps strengthen the pair bond before they settle down to breed, constructing their floating nest out of waterweed and other vegetation close to the edge of the loch.

Also known as the 'Horned Grebe' because of those bright orange tufts of feathers on the sides of its head, the Slavonian Grebe is now sadly in rapid decline as a British breeding bird.

THE BIG MELT

Up on the high tops of the Cairngorm plateau, south to the Great Glen and across to the western Highlands, thick snow still covers the ground; it will remain at least until May, and possibly even later. But the narrow streams and rivulets that run down off the mountains into the valleys below are now filling up with clear, icy water – a sign that the Big Melt is finally under way. It remains bitterly cold – especially on clear, cloudless nights – but spring and the breeding season are showing definite signs of appearing.

On a cliff ledge on the north-eastern face of a steep, rocky crag, a Golden Eagle is sitting. A few weeks ago she returned to this site – where she and her partner nested last year – to check it out and make sure that nothing had changed in the intervening few months to make it unsuitable for them to breed again this spring.

She added more sticks to the already vast nest. Golden Eagle eyries are usually about 1.3 m (4 ft) long, 1 m (3 ft) wide and 80 cm (2½ ft) deep, and can weigh as much as 250 kg (550 lb). The largest Golden Eagle nest ever found, in the US state of Montana, was an incredible 2.6 m (8½ ft) wide and more than 6 m (20 ft) deep.

The vast majority of Golden Eagles in the Highlands nest on ledges on cliffs and crags, whereas elsewhere in the world (and occasionally in Scotland) they prefer tall trees such as pines. The nest site is usually about halfway up the mountainside, so that the adults can bring back heavier prey such as Mountain Hares more easily than if they were breeding at the very top. The nest does need to be high enough to keep the eggs and chicks safe from predators and intruders, which in the absence of large mammals such as Wolves mainly means humans.

Golden Eagles begin nesting very early in the New Year; by springtime they usually have two chicks in their nest known as an 'eyrie'.

Most eyries are built facing north or east, to avoid the young birds overheating on hot days.

This particular eyrie is facing north-east, which may seem odd given the prevailing climate, but the majority of Golden Eagle nests have a northerly or easterly aspect, as strong sunlight can cause the youngsters to become dehydrated and die. This is not the only nest this pair has made. Typically Golden Eagles build two to five eyries during their lifetimes, giving them the option to choose one over another depending on the conditions in any particular year.

Having checked out the eyrie, added some twigs to it and chosen it for this breeding season, the pair of eagles wasted no time in getting started. After mating the female laid two large eggs at the start of March – a dirty shade of creamy-white, speckled and blotched with reddish-brown – and she and her mate are now incubating, a task that will take just over six weeks before the first egg finally hatches.

Unlike the songbirds now sitting on eggs in the valley below, Golden Eagles do not wait until the whole clutch of eggs is laid before they begin incubating. Instead they start to sit as soon as the first of (usually) two eggs has been laid. This is common among birds of prey and owls, and has evolved as a kind of 'insurance policy' against a shortage of food – as we shall discover later in the season. In the meantime the male and female share the duties of incubation, and when not sitting on the nest either perch nearby, standing guard, or fly off on their huge, broad wings to search for food, often many miles from their eyrie.

SPRING MAKEOVER

For the three 'snow-white' creatures of the high tops, March and April can be a tricky time of year. During the winter the Ptarmigan, Mountain Hare and Stoat have turned almost entirely white; the first two to avoid predators such as the Golden Eagle, and the last to conceal itself as it tries to catch its prey – which includes the Ptarmigan and Mountain Hare.

The timing of when each of these mammals chooses to shed its white winter garb and adopt a new appearance for the arrival of spring depends on a number of factors. As is the case with many seasonal changes for birds, such as migration and breeding, one of these is light. The increasing day length may be gradual, but is nevertheless triggering crucial chemical changes in the brains of birds and mammals, one of which triggers the process of moult.

The prevailing weather, especially the snow conditions, is also important. In a very late spring, with thick snow lying on the ground well into May, both the Ptarmigan and Mountain Hare may delay their moult, retaining the white plumage that protects them so well. If spring comes early and the snow begins to melt sooner than usual, the change may begin earlier. In any case, different individuals show very different appearances at this time of year.

In spring, a Mountain Hare is barely recognisable as the same creature we saw in the winter, having moulted its white coat into grey-brown, to remain camouflaged as the snow melts.

The Stoat has also changed its appearance, swapping the white of winter for the more familiar chestnut-brown and buff combination of spring, summer and autumn.

OVERLEAF *Red-throated Divers* live up to their name from spring onwards, when they return from their winter quarters off the coast to the lochs across the Highlands, where they breed.

The male Ptarmigan turns a rich gold and chestnut, with white underparts, dark blotches on its head and neck, and a bright red eyebrow; the female sports a more uniform golden-brown shade, enabling her to stay camouflaged on the nest. By April the Ptarmigan have left their winter flocks and paired up. The male often calls to defend his territory against rivals, and the hillsides echo with his distinctive croaking voice.

The Mountain Hares are changing colour too, moulting from the white winter coat into a patchwork of blotchy grey and white, which can still offer surprisingly good camouflage against a backdrop of snow patches and rocky scree. They too are pairing up to breed, and although a few leverets may appear as early as March, the majority of the first of up to three litters is born in April or May.

Stoats are always on the lookout for food, and at this time of year any newly born young hares are a welcome and easily caught item of prey. Stoats too will often retain their winter coats for as long as they can, as even in May this will enable them to hide among patches of snow. Gradually the brown summer coat will start to show, giving the animals a rather blotchy appearance until their moult is fully complete.

The female Stoat patiently stalking a pair of Ptarmigan is, although you might not realise it from looking at her, already pregnant with a litter of young, known as kits. She mated last June but, like some other mammals, she is able to delay implanting the fertilised egg, in her case by as long as ten months, so that the actual pregnancy only lasts four weeks. In a few days she will give birth to 6–12 kits, which like many young mammals are born deaf, blind and naked.

Birds and mammals may be the most obvious of the inhabitants of these high tops, but they are not the only creatures found here. Reptiles and amphibians may be less easy to see, but they are just as active as their larger cousins, especially in spring. On the moors and in the forest rides, Adders are emerging from their long winter hibernation. On sunny spring days they flatten their bodies in order to make the warming process as efficient as possible, before heading off to find food.

On the slopes themselves small pools and lochans may contain Common Frog tadpoles, which were hatched last year, not this year. That's because the temperatures are so low here that the tadpoles are not able to grow and develop into frogs in a single season; it takes up to two years for this process to be complete.

SHOWING OFF IN THE FOREST

As dawn breaks in the Caledonian pine forests, a very different chorus echoes through these ancient trees. It's not the melodious sound of songbirds, but the grunts, whistles and pops that make up the courtship display of one of our biggest and most impressive breeding birds: the Capercaillie.

A male Capercaillie is a pretty incredible bird. The world's largest grouse, with males weighing in at more than 4 kg (9 lb), it looks rather like a cross between a pheasant and a turkey. In the pre-dawn light of March or April it appears black at a distance, but a closer look reveals purples, mauves and browns, a scarlet eyebrow, ivory-coloured bill and black tail, which is held fanned above the head like that of a strutting Peacock. The male is displaying to impress a bevy of watching females – smaller (at less than half his weight), browner and far less impressive. They have gathered at this displaying arena – known as a lek (see box below) – to watch him as he struts up and down, all the while uttering bizarre sounds.

The sight of a displaying male Capercaillie is striking, but is rivalled by the bird's amazing sound, which has been compared to the recording of a bottle of champagne being opened – but played backwards, so that the glugging of the liquid being poured ends with the loud popping of the cork leaving the bottle.

The beautiful Twinflower is a relic of the Ice Age and is now a rare plant in Scotland. Its range closely matches that of the Caledonian pine forest, home of the Capercaillie.

*he male Capercaillie is one
f Britain's most magnificent
•irds, though sadly now also
ne of our most critically
ndangered.*

Sadly, we are hearing this sound less and less often in the Highlands, for the Capercaillie is in big trouble, and not for the first time in its chequered history as a British bird. Having been here since prehistoric times – there are fossil records from 150,000 years ago – it was driven to extinction in Britain during the Middle Ages. This was mainly because of the destruction of the vast pine forests, but also because it was large, easy to catch and good to eat.

During the 1830s Capercaillies from the Scandinavian population were brought back to Britain, and for a while they thrived. By the early 20th century the species could be found across much of the Highlands, and even as recently as 1970 there were estimated to be 20,000 individuals. However, during the 1980s and 1990s three factors coincided in a 'perfect storm' to drive down Capercaillie numbers. First, the Forestry Commission planted dense plantations of Sitka Spruce on many hillsides, where Red Deer usually spend the winter. This forced the deer into the pinewoods for shelter, where they destroyed the forest understorey, so that Capercaillie chicks had nowhere to hide – especially from opportunistic Hooded Crows.

To try to combat this problem, the Forestry Commission then erected fences inside the woods to control the deer movements. While this made ecological sense in one respect, it was a major problem for low-flying Capercaillies – so much so that collisions with the fences became the number one killer of adult birds. Meanwhile, the shooting community developed 'caper stalking' – tracking down and shooting large 'trophy cocks', which became especially popular with rich Belgian and Italian hunters.

A series of cool, wet springs in the past few years has continued to devastate Capercaillie numbers. Young chicks are especially vulnerable to wet weather from April to June, as they follow their mother through the vegetation and easily become waterlogged, rapidly freezing to death.

The welcome increase in the Pine Marten population may also be causing problems for the Capercaillie, for this adaptable predator can easily find the nests and eggs of any ground-nesting bird. Nor do Capercaillies live very long: the chicks have only a 50-50 chance of surviving their first year, and the oldest recorded Capercaillie died at just three and a half years old. Today there may be fewer than 1,200 of these majestic birds remaining, and as numbers continue to fall the Capercaillie may once again be doomed to disappear from Scotland – which really would be a tragedy.

Leks

Lekking is one of the most bizarre of all behaviours in nature. The name lek derives from a Scandinavian word meaning 'play', which is highly appropriate given the dramatic nature of the performance. Two species found in the Highlands, the Capercaillie and Black Grouse, perform at leks during the breeding season, as does a more common wader, the Woodcock.

For lekking to occur a specific set of factors needs to be in place – notably that the food which these birds eat is found across a broad area, so that the males do not have to spend time defending a territory against rivals.

Both Capercaillies and Black Grouse feed on a wide range of plant material, including pine needles, heather shoots and berries; Capercaillies also eat small pine cones. All these are abundant and widely available, so that instead of fighting to defend their food supply, male Capercaillies and Black Grouse (known as blackcocks) can indulge in what at first seems to be rather odd behaviour.

The Black Grouse lek is even more complicated than that of the Capercaillie, as it involves up to a dozen males. Just before dawn they gather on the lekking site, each taking up its place depending on its position as far as dominance goes; the strongest males go to the centre of the lek. Then the birds fight – well not fight, exactly, but indulge in scuffles and squabbles, leaping up in the air and holding out their claws, flapping their wings and all the while uttering a strange series of pigeon-like cooing sounds.

The whole spectacle can appear rather comical, but of course it is deadly serious, for the winning male gets to mate with the majority of females – just as in the Red Deer rut that takes place later in the year.

FOREST SONGBIRDS

More conventional breeding behaviour than that of the Capercaillie and Black Grouse continues all over the forest. The Scottish Crossbills we saw in February – one of the earliest of all Britain's birds to begin breeding – successfully hatched their brood of four chicks towards the end of the month. These fledged into their first 'proper' plumage and left the nest three weeks later, in mid-March, and since then both parents have kept a close eye on them, feeding them pine-cone seeds. If the weather stays good, the female may lay a second clutch of eggs, but for the moment she is busy looking after her first set of offspring.

The other special songbird of these forests, the Crested Tit, is also well into its breeding cycle, although not quite so advanced as the crossbills. One pair has now chosen a dead birch stump as a nest-site, and having dug out the rotten wood at the top to form a cavity, the female laid her clutch of six eggs – white with dark red spots – in early April. These now nestle in a soft cup of moss lined with mammal fur and feathers.

The female hides away in the cavity from any danger, only occasionally leaving to grab a morsel of food, aware that predators such as Pine Martens and Red Squirrels may be watching close by. She incubates the clutch for two weeks, and her chicks – born, like all songbirds, naked, blind and helpless – grow rapidly as both parents bring back food constantly during every hour of daylight. Finally, after three weeks, they leave the nest, but just like the young Scottish Crossbills they stay with their parents for another three weeks or so before they are fully independent.

The Crested Tit nests, like the commoner and more familiar members of its family, in holes or crevices in trees.

FIONA SMITH ⋯ REINDEER MANAGER

Fiona was born and brought up in the Highlands and works in the family business – Cairngorm Reindeer – with her parents, Alan and Tilly, and brother Alex. The whole of her childhood revolved around these magnificent animals, and although her parents didn't pressure her to work there, she feels it was meant to be. Showing people the Reindeer is always a pleasure for Fiona, especially as they are so friendly and so much a part of the landscape up on the Cairngorm Mountains.

Fiona's work certainly isn't over once the daily Reindeer tour has finished. These animals are free range, so she often has to walk miles across the hills in search of them. In May – the calving season – she is kept busy welcoming new Reindeer into the herd. Leading up to Christmas, she also takes some animals to meet people in towns up and down the country. She never has time to get bored – the job is ever changing.

What Fiona likes most about the Reindeer is that they are both very tame, yet at the same time they can be so wild. Even though she and the visitors can get in among these tame animals each day, later on when the people all head back to their nice warm homes and hotels, the Reindeer remain up there whatever the weather.

Of all the four seasons, Fiona prefers autumn. Partly this is because of the spectacular colours – the purple of the heather, and the yellows, browns and oranges of the trees – but also because this is the time of year when the Reindeer are looking their very best. They have gone through the summer fattening up and growing beautiful antlers, so are at their absolute prime.

Although Fiona has a deep love for the Reindeer she looks after, another favourite creature is a tiny bird, the Snow Bunting. She is sure that they have learnt the call Fiona and her colleagues use to attract the Reindeer, because whenever they go out to feed the animals in winter a little flock of Snow Buntings turns up, too, waiting patiently to pick up any leftovers.

Fiona's favourite place in the Highlands has to be the Cairngorm Mountains – her office and her playground. Even though the weather can be pretty bad, for her that is what makes this place so special: 'The worse the weather, the more you really appreciate the wildness.'

UP IN THE CANOPY

Birds aren't the only creatures getting down to the serious business of breeding in the Caledonian pine forests. Mammals, too, take advantage of longer hours of daylight and abundant supplies of food to raise a family at this time of year.

For the Red Squirrel hopping acrobatically from branch to branch above the Crested Tit's nest, this is also a crucial time, for she has made repairs to her drey high in the canopy of a tall Scots Pine, and is now preparing to give birth to a litter of three young. It's been a good year so far; the weather wasn't too bad during the winter, so she has managed to keep her body weight high enough to breed – had it fallen below about 300 g (10½ oz) she wouldn't have become fertile this season.

The male squirrel is nowhere to be seen. Having done his parental duty by mating with the female earlier in the year, he has nothing to do with raising his offspring; indeed, he will now be looking out for more females to impregnate.

Like baby songbirds, Red Squirrels are born naked, deaf and blind. Hairs begin to emerge through the skin after eight or nine days, and by the time the babies are three weeks old they are fully covered with fur. However, they won't be able to see or hear until they are at least four or perhaps five weeks old. They'll remain in the safety of the drey for about seven weeks in all, but will stay close to their mother, alternating between feeding on her milk and on solid food.

Few animals are so closely associated with the Highland forests as the Red Squirrel, which nests, sleeps and feeds amongst Scots Pines.

Pine Martens, like the other mammals of the Highlands, give birth in spring when plenty of food is available for their young.

The female Pine Marten taking a close look at the Crested Tit as she goes to and from the nest with food for her young is also about to give birth. She mated long ago – sometime last summer – but just like her cousin the Stoat has delayed implanting the fertilised egg so that she gives birth the following spring.

She will also give birth to three young – Pine Martens can have 2–6 offspring, which each weigh just 30 g (1 oz). Like the baby squirrels they are born blind, and remain so until they are over a month old. Unlike the squirrels, however, Pine Martens are born covered with a layer of whitish fur, which gradually develops into the familiar brown-and-yellow coat while they are in the den.

The Scottish Wildcat, the third member of this mammal trio – and by far the rarest – is also giving birth in this spring period. Wildcats produce a single litter of three or four kittens each year, and these too are blind when they are born, but covered with fur. Their weight at birth can vary considerably, from about 65 g to over 160 g (2–6 oz), but those born below 90 g (3 oz) usually do not survive.

The kittens open their eyes at one or two weeks old, revealing their dazzling blue colour, which later changes to the familiar glowing green usually associated with this species. As they grow they become more and more active, walking and playing with one another, but always staying close to their mother unless she is away hunting for food.

DUCK DISPLAYS

A month or so ago, on a fine day at the end of February, a pair of Goldeneyes began its courtship ritual on a remote loch in the eastern Highlands. The male tentatively approached the female, threw his head over his back, and started to emit a series of strange, buzzing and to some ears rather mechanical sounds – this handsome duck's equivalent of birdsong.

True to form, like most female ducks his prospective mate was having none of it. Each time he came near she turned away, swimming in the opposite direction with him following frantically in pursuit. The commotion attracted a second male, then a third, until all three were harassing the poor duck, which eventually tired of all the attention and flew away. Later, however, the male's advances must have worked, for now, in early April, they are a couple.

Fifty years ago that would have been that, at least as far as local observers were concerned. Having paired up, both male and female Goldeneyes, along with the rest of their clan, would have headed north-east to breed in the vast forests and lakes of Scandinavia or northern Russia. However, from the early 1970s onwards Goldeneyes in the Scottish Highlands changed their habits. Along with several other northern species, instead of just spending the winter here and breeding further north, they chose to stay put on this side of the North Sea all year round. So while Scottish Goldeneyes now mostly head to the coast for the winter, they return in early spring to breed in the Highlands.

The Goldeneye is one of the great success stories of recent years. Having colonised the Highlands in the early 1970s it is now thriving, thanks partly to the provision of nestboxes for the birds to breed.

Male and female Goldeneyes could hardly be more different in appearance. The male (top) is mainly black and white, while the female (bottom) is grey with a chestnut head.

They do so thanks to some far-sighted thinking by local birders and ornithologists. When the Goldeneye decided to stay to breed all those years ago, these people realised that this tree-nesting species didn't have enough places to nest; there simply weren't enough suitably sized holes. So they provided the next best thing: wooden nestboxes, which the Goldeneye took to like, well, a duck to water. As a result, today there are perhaps 150 to 200 nesting pairs of Goldeneye in Scotland, mostly in Strathspey, but with some also in Aberdeenshire and a few all the way south to the Borders.

Watching this pair of Goldeneye swimming on a glassy loch, it strikes you just how beautiful a monochrome bird can be. The female is attractive enough, with her pearl-grey body and dark chestnut-brown head. But her mate is a real stunner, with a strikingly delineated black-and-white plumage, his bulbous black head gleaming with a green sheen when the sun shines. The sun also reflects that bright golden eye – the feature that gives the duck its name.

The male may have been attentive during the courtship period, but he doesn't hang around for long afterwards. For almost a month, while the female incubates her clutch of 8–11 eggs, he is nowhere to be seen. When the youngsters are ready to leave the nest, just 24 hours after hatching, she jumps out first and sits below, encouraging them to leap with soft, reassuring calls. Once all are safely on the ground she leads them to water, where like all baby ducks they begin to feed immediately, driven by an instinctive understanding of how to dive and catch their tiny invertebrate prey. They stay with their mother for about seven weeks, but on a fine day in late May or June they will head off by themselves. Even then, they may not be able to fly for another week or so, during which they are very vulnerable to being attacked by predators.

THE OTTER'S RETURN

Along with the Golden Eagle and Scottish Wildcat, Otters are one of the apex predators of the Highlands, so called because of their place at the very top of the food chain. A healthy population of apex predators is essential for a healthy and functioning ecosystem, and the Highlands is no exception. So it's good news that Otters are doing very well indeed – not just on the river systems such as the Spey and Dee, but also around the coasts.

Otters that live by the coast sometimes get called sea otters, which can cause confusion with the different (though related) species of Sea Otter living along the Pacific coasts of North America. In fact the Otters we see along the east and west coasts that border the Highlands are the same species – *Lutra lutra*, the European Otter – that can be found throughout Britain, whether on rivers or on the coast.

Coastal Otters do behave somewhat differently, however. Otters are usually nocturnal or crepuscular (active at dawn and dusk), but like any animal they will go where the food is. For an Otter living on the coast the availability of food is dependent not on the 24-hour cycle of day and night, but on that of the tides. This means that whatever the time of day, you always have a chance of seeing an Otter along the coast – especially if you spot it before it sees you, as Otters can be very shy and wary of humans. This is for good reason – Otters were ruthlessly persecuted for centuries, as they take fish that our ancestors wanted for themselves. Later, pursuing them turned into a blood sport, and they were hunted with packs of specially bred Otterhounds. Fortunately this grisly pastime was finally banned in the late 20th century, and since then Otters have bounced back. But even in the darkest days of the 1950s and 1960s, when Otters virtually disappeared from England and Wales, they still found a safe refuge in the more remote and isolated parts of the Highlands, and especially along the western coasts, where the bays and beaches proved ideal for this adaptable animal.

The coasts around the Highlands are the ideal habitat for the Otter, though they have to change their daily cycle to suit the changes in the tides, rather than being mainly nocturnal, like their river-dwelling cousins.

The Otter is perfectly adapted for a life spent partly in the water and partly on land, with a thick fur coat and sleek, streamlined body enabling it to swim and run.

The first sight of an Otter along the coastline usually comes when you notice a V-shaped line in the water, followed by a long trail of bubbles. Look out for the appearance of a sleek, smooth head and bewhiskered face. Then, if you are lucky, you'll see the whole animal as it leaves the comparative safety of the water and trots along the rocky beach. Otters are often found where there is seaweed just offshore, as this harbours the food they are looking for: fish, crustaceans such as crabs, and anything else they can find.

A swimming Otter can be momentarily mistaken for a seal, but Otters are much smaller and more slender, and once ashore have a very distinctive style of running, as the back lifts into the air while they trot along on short legs, trailing their long, broad tail behind them.

Otters – especially females – are very territorial, and often have quite a large home range, along 5–14 km (3–9 miles) of coastline. Males are less tied to one place than females, and often wander quite long distances in search of food or the opportunity to mate. Just like river Otters, coastal Otters build a holt, digging tunnels inland from the shore, where they rest up when not feeding or, in the case of the female, give birth and raise their young.

Both males and females use their faeces (known as spraints) to mark their territory, and also to communicate with one another; they also whistle, grunt and chirp. If they do meet, the encounters are often quite aggressive, with frequent fights that can easily result in injury or even death to the weaker party – often the smaller female.

Otters mate at any time of year, but usually give birth to two or perhaps three cubs from May onwards. These stay in the holt at first, but grow very quickly and are able to swim when they reach three months old. However, they remain with their mother for the rest of the year, learning how to find food so that when they become independent they are better able to survive.

One beautiful spot on the west coast of Scotland, Sandaig Bay, near the village of Glenelg, was immortalised as 'Camusfearna' by author and naturalist Gavin Maxwell in his 1960 novel *Ring of Bright Water*. The story tells of how he raised pet otters here, although these were not our native Scottish variety, but Smooth-coated Otters (a separate, slightly smaller species), which the author had brought back from his travels to the marshes of Iraq. The book became a massive bestseller, whose fame increased when it was turned into a film starring Bill Travers and Virginia McKenna a decade later.

Today, you can still see native Otters in the bay by Maxwell's former home, along with a pair of White-tailed (Sea) Eagles that have also taken up residence at this beautiful and tranquil spot.

WATCHING THE RIVER FLOW

Back on the River Spey, by late April spring is in full flow. Three small but distinctive bird species are taking advantage of a plentiful supply of aquatic invertebrates to raise their families along the river's banks.

If you take a walk upstream from Nethy Bridge, or indeed any of the crossings over the Spey, you may hear a thin, piercing, high-pitched call. Look along the river and the chances are that you'll see a slender, long-tailed bird disappearing into the distance. It's a male Grey Wagtail.

Despite its name, this really is one of our most beautiful birds. It has a steel-grey head, back and wings, and jet-black throat contrasting with the lemon-yellow underparts – so bright that this species is often mistaken for its cousin the Yellow Wagtail, a summer visitor to southern Britain. But if you see a 'yellow' wagtail in Scotland, especially along a river, the chances are that it's a Grey Wagtail.

Look carefully as you head along the path alongside the river and you may catch sight of the bird perched on water-sprayed rocks, its tail frantically pumping up and down. It's looking for tiny insects – usually flies and midges – that it catches by launching itself into the air and grabbing them with its pointed bill, before returning to land.

Grey Wagtails usually build their nest in a hole or crevice under an old stone bridge, where they can easily fly in and out but which predators cannot reach. They lay 4–6 eggs, which they incubate for as short a time as any British bird – just 11 days. The youngsters fledge and leave the nest after another couple of weeks, but may continue to return there as a place of refuge whenever they feel unsafe.

Highland rivers, like the River Spey, are home to a wide range of wild creatures, from birds to mammals and insects to amphibians.

The Dipper is Britain's only aquatic songbird, spending the whole of its life along a short stretch of fast-flowing river.

Another bird often seen along these rivers, and which also bobs up and down while searching for food, is the Common Sandpiper. Like the Grey Wagtail it too has a high-pitched call, and also perches on water-soaked rocks while looking for food. Unlike the wagtail it nests on the ground, usually in vegetation close to the riverbank. With dark head and upperparts and white underparts, and a short, straight beak, it is easy to identify, especially as no other waders habitually live in this riverine habitat at this time of the year.

The final member of this water-loving trio is another songbird, although in shape and habits it looks more like a wader. This is the Dipper, a bird distantly related to Wrens and thrushes, but which has adapted completely to an aquatic lifestyle.

Dippers are plump little birds about the size of a Starling, but with a pot belly and cocked tail making them look rather like giant Wrens. They are dark above, but the most obvious feature is the white patch on the underparts, which is often the first thing you catch sight of as the bird bobs up and down on distant rocks. Why the Dipper – and indeed these other river specialists – chooses to behave in such a way is a bit of a mystery. It's most likely that this activity helps break up the bird's outline to any potential prey looking up from the river below.

Dippers dive into the water to get food – rather like a Kingfisher, although less spectacularly – but they also walk along the bottom of a river as they hunt for small creatures hidden in the stones along its bed. They build a nest in a crevice in a bank, making the nest very vulnerable to flooding, and raise 4–5 young that, like the young Grey Wagtails, also return to the nest to roost in the weeks after fledging.

Unlike Grey Wagtails and Common Sandpipers, both of which leave the river after the breeding season is over (the Common Sandpiper heads all the way to Africa), the Dipper stays put here all year round. Indeed, Dippers are one of the most sedentary of all Highland birds, rarely venturing more than a couple of kilometres from where they breed, although juvenile birds may travel a little further during their first year of life.

OUT OF AFRICA

The Osprey is not the only species to have come back from Africa, although it is usually one of the first to arrive. Week by week, throughout April and May, more and more migrants return to the Highlands, and take their places in the meadows, woods, lakes, rivers and mountains that make up this unique landscape.

Perhaps the most pervasive sound heard in the birch woods around the lochs is the song of our most common summer visitor, the Willow Warbler. Unlike the Swallow, Swift and House Martin, this may not be a very familiar species, yet with well over 2 million pairs breeding in Britain, it comfortably outnumbers them all.

The Willow Warbler's song can be heard from the middle of April onwards: a silvery cascade of notes running down the scale, with a rather plaintive, wistful tone. The bird itself is at first sight rather nondescript: about the size of a Blue Tit, although slimmer. It is pale green below with darker, brownish-green upperparts, and with a dark stripe running through the eye and a more noticeable pale stripe just above.

Like all small warblers Willow Warblers are active little birds, constantly flitting about the foliage in search of tiny insects on which they feed.

This little bird may weigh just 10 g (⅓ oz) – about the same as the smaller but stockier Wren – but it undergoes one of the longest and most arduous global journeys of any of our songbirds. Each autumn Willow Warblers travel all the way to southern Africa and back, a round trip of almost 20,000 km (12,400 miles). To do so they need long, slender wings – a useful aid to identification, as their very similar-looking relative the Chiffchaff has much shorter wings, giving it a less streamlined appearance.

The Willow Warbler (top) and Wheatear (bottom) are two long-distance migrant songbirds, which return to Scotland from sub-Saharan Africa each spring.

he juvenile Cuckoo never
eets its parents, yet still
anages to travel thousands
f miles to Africa on its own,
eeks after fledging.

Virtually uniquely amongst songbirds, the Willow Warbler moults not once, but twice each year: once in its African winter quarters, then again on its breeding grounds after it has bred. We are not quite sure why it does this, although the fact that it has to travel so far may be the reason – freshly moulted feathers enable the bird to fly more efficiently.

Willow Warblers have declined dramatically in the southern parts of their breeding range, including southern England, perhaps because conditions there are becoming less suitable for the species due to global warming. However, in the Highlands their distinctive song can be heard from April until June, a permanent soundtrack accompanying any walk through the deciduous forests.

Another species doing well in the Highlands, yet declining elsewhere, is the Cuckoo – perhaps the best known of all our summer visitors, at least from its sound, even if the bird itself is harder to see than hear. Cuckoos return from late April onwards, and after mating the females lay their eggs – up to 20 in all –

in the nests of their host species. In the case of Scottish Cuckoos, the hosts are mostly Meadow Pipits on the open moors.

After hatching a young Cuckoo ejects any chicks or remaining eggs from the nest, so that it has the full and undivided attention of its unfortunate foster parents, which then spend every waking hour bringing back large, hairy caterpillars and other insects for their hungry 'offspring'.

The Willow Warbler and Cuckoo aren't the only summer migrants doing rather better in the Scottish Highlands than further south. Whinchats, Wood Warblers and especially Spotted Flycatchers are fairly common and widespread here in May and June, while in England and Wales they are struggling to survive , and have disappeared from many of their former haunts. The reason for this appears to be that a reliable supply of insects, on which these species – and especially their hungry chicks – depend, is still widely available in the Highlands, where most farming is still much less intensive than it is down south.

The Corncrake's comeback

Traditional farming is a crucial factor in the survival of another summer visitor to Scotland, the Corncrake – a species that was once found all over rural Britain, but that is now confined as a British breeding bird to the Scottish Highlands and Islands.

Also known as the Landrail (to distinguish it from its wetland-dwelling cousin the Water Rail), the Corncrake was once the quintessential bird of the lowland farmed countryside throughout the whole of Britain. However, during the 19th and early 20th centuries, as farming became more and more mechanised, the bird began a steady and inexorable decline.

The Corncrake's scientific name, *Crex crex*, derives from its extraordinary call: a repetitive, two-note, grating sound, which the bird makes throughout the night – and often all day as well – when it is breeding. You are far more likely to hear the Corncrake than to see it, for it hides deep in the dense vegetation, only rarely emerging for a few moments at a time.

The shape of a Moorhen, although slightly smaller and slimmer, the Corncrake has sandy-brown plumage marked with russet and black, a grey face and head, and a short yellowish bill. When flushed it shows small russet wings, which hardly look strong enough to carry the bird into the next field, yet nevertheless are used for an epic journey south to Africa and back.

At one point it seemed as if we might lose the Corncrake as a British breeding bird. Fortunately, however, at the eleventh hour the RSPB stepped in, and has worked with local crofters and farmers to enable them to farm the land sympathetically for this very special bird. Thanks to this scheme, Corncrake numbers have boomed. From an all-time low of fewer than 500 pairs, the population in Scotland has now risen to more than 1,200 pairs.

ROLE REVERSAL ON THE HIGH TOPS

Meadows, forests and sea cliffs are where you might expect to find a summer visitor such as the Corncrake, Willow Warbler and Puffin. However, there is one migrant that returns from North Africa each year not to the Isle of Skye or the Spey Valley, but to the high tops of the Cairngorm plateau.

The high tops of the Cairngorm plateau may still have patches of snow well into spring and even early summer.

This is a wader – although unlike plovers and sandpipers it doesn't spend its time wading. It is also one of only two species of British breeding bird in which the usual roles are reversed, with the female taking the lead in courtship and the male doing all the work to raise a family. It's name means 'stupid bird', yet it can be remarkably adaptable. It is the Dotterel.

The Dotterel is a striking and very beautiful bird. A little larger than a Ringed Plover and noticeably smaller than the Golden Plover (although similar in shape), the brighter female has a rusty-orange belly, with a narrow white stripe dividing this from the grey breast; a white throat, black cap and eye-stripe, with a white band above the eye; scalloped brown upperparts; a short bill and yellow legs. The male is similar in appearance although slightly less brightly coloured.

To see this rare wader – only about 600 pairs breed here each summer – you need to visit the high tops of the Highlands from early May through to July or August, when the birds start to head south again. For such striking birds Dotterels can be surprisingly elusive, but once you have spotted one they are usually fairly easy to approach – hence their reputation for being stupid. However, it is always advisable to keep your distance during the breeding season, as if you distract them you could make it easier for predators to seize their eggs or chicks.

Having mated and laid her clutch of two or three eggs in a shallow scrape in the ground, lined with moss or lichen, the female Dotterel doesn't usually stay around for long. Indeed, some females fly all the way across the North Sea to Norway, to mate again with a different male during the same breeding season. Meanwhile the male assiduously incubates his clutch for up to four weeks, then looks after the fluffy chicks for another month, although they are able to feed themselves almost from birth. Dotterel eat a wide range of insects and other invertebrates, including craneflies and their larvae, spiders, flies and beetles – anything they can find on the high tops.

Unusually amongst birds, the male Dotterel is less bright and showy than the female, and takes on all the incubation and chick-rearing duties.

ALL CHANGE – AGAIN

Towards the time the young Dotterel are fledging and becoming independent, in the middle of June, the resident creatures of the mountain plateau are enjoying the benefits of seemingly endless hours of daylight and a plentiful supply of food.

A young Mountain Hare, known as a leveret, is perfectly camouflaged for avoiding predators.

The Ptarmigan now look very different from how they did at the start of the breeding season, when they were beginning to moult out of their white winter garb. Now, as the female sits tightly on her clutch of half a dozen eggs, she is a mottled brownish-grey in colour, blending in perfectly with the lichen-covered rocks and bare ground. You can sometimes spot her mate by looking out for his bright crimson eyebrows; otherwise he too blends in remarkably well.

The Mountain Hares may by now be onto their second litter. Any surviving offspring born in March are fully independent, but the new leverets are still totally reliant on their parents for food and protection. A scan across a boulder-strewn landscape may reveal that some of the distant grey objects you assumed were rocks are actually Mountain Hares; or, of course, vice versa.

The Stoat shed his ermine winter coat long ago. He too has a family to feed: as many as 13 hungry kits, for which he catches hares and Ptarmigan, voles and shrews, or takes a clutch of bird's eggs. Incredibly, while the youngsters are still in the nest a rival male Stoat may come and mate with the female kits, so that by the time they mature into adults they are already expecting their first litter.

Young Golden Eagles stay in the nest for about ten weeks, before they fledge and leave.

Meanwhile, back at the Golden Eagle eyrie, the two chicks are unrecognisable from the tiny, fluffy creatures of a few weeks ago. Although the elder of the two is developing well, and is now close to fledging and leaving the nest, his younger sibling is looking far less healthy. Indeed, he is now at a crucial point in his development, for if he fails to get enough food during the next couple of weeks, he will die.

In the case of the vast majority of bird species, his survival would be mainly dependent on one thing: the ability of his parents to catch and bring back enough food to the nest. But for Golden Eagles things are very different. Even if the male and female do bring back plenty of food, the older sibling may keep it all for himself, actively preventing the younger, weaker chick from feeding.

This phenomenon – shown by most species of large eagle around the world – is known as Cain and Abel Syndrome, or simply Cainism, after the story in the Old Testament Book of Genesis in which Adam's son Cain murdered his brother Abel. Although we might recoil at what appears to be a ruthless, deliberate killing, it's important to understand that this is driven by the logic of survival. If both chicks are fed equally, at times of food shortages both may prove too weak to survive.

By delaying the hatching of the second egg the parents are hedging their bets. At times of plenty, when prey is easy to find, both chicks do survive, but otherwise only the elder and stronger one makes it. However, eagle scientist Jeff Watson has pointed out that even at times when food is abundant the older chick may still show aggression towards its sibling, eventually leading to the smaller chick's death. This shows just how powerful the instinct to survive can be.

Cainism appears to be more frequent in the western Highlands, probably because there is less food available, although this is not the case on Skye, where there are plenty of Rabbits and seabirds to feed the young.

Therefore sometime during the ten-week period between hatching and fledging, the younger chick normally dies from starvation, aggression or more usually a combination of both. The survivor, which when it hatched weighed just 100 g (4 oz), now weighs in at 3.5 kg (8 lb); female eaglets are even heavier, at 4 kg (9 lb). He remains with his parents – and depends on them for food – for another three months. Only when the autumn winds begin to blow, sometime in October, does he finally become independent and head off to hunt for himself.

Significant Highlanders

JOHN LISTER-KAYE ⋯ WRITER AND NATURALIST

John Lister-Kaye is one of the most respected and admired conservationists and nature writers in Britain. Thousands of people pass each year through the gates of the Aigas Field Centre, which he founded 40 years ago, while tens of thousands read his magical books. However, he arrived in the Highlands almost by accident.

A Yorkshireman by birth, John was lured northwards by Gavin Maxwell's 1960 novel *Ring of Bright Water*. Eight years later he moved permanently to the Highlands to work with Maxwell, and after the author's tragic early death John decided to stay in Scotland to lead guided wildlife tours. In 1976 he started running courses at Aigas, near the town of Beauly, which today is one of the most visited field centres in the UK, and provides environmental education for 6,000 Highland schoolchildren and 750 visiting adults every year.

John knows he is very lucky to have realised his dream of living in the Highlands and showing their unique wildlife to others. He loves working with the team of dedicated young rangers at the centre, and entertaining the guests in Aigas's unique dining hall.

Spring is John's favourite season by far – as he points out, the winter at Aigas lasts for seven months, so they long for the spring! It brings the display flight of his favourite bird, the Lapwing, with its stunning colours and plaintive, evocative calls. His favourite Highlands mammal, the Weasel, is less easy to see. He also has a soft spot for the Horntail Wood Wasp, a stunningly beautiful insect whose long ovipositor looks like a wasp's sting.

In 40 years, John has seen plenty of changes in the Highlands. Not all of them have been welcome, such as the electricity pylons that now spoil the view from his home. However, he still believes that the Highlands are an immensely rewarding place to visit, with what he calls 'a palpable sense of wildness'.

Moreover, when John wants to get away for a while, he can simply head up the hill to his favourite place, the Iron Age fort at Aigas, which boasts stunning views over Strathglass and, in spring and summer, sunbathing Adders. He doesn't have to go that far, though, to see wildlife – Red Squirrels and Pine Martens live in the grounds of his home, and he is able to watch Golden Eagles from the comfort of his bed.

THE TOUGHEST BUTTERFLY OF ALL?

When the last ice age ended 10,000 years ago and the ice sheets that covered much of Britain finally – and it seems permanently – retreated to the north, Britain's butterflies gradually began to recolonise from the south. Almost all of these would have been eliminated during the ice age itself. Familiar species such as the Red Admiral and Small Tortoiseshell would simply have been unable to survive in this barren landscape of tundra, permafrost and – on the higher parts of Britain, including the Scottish Highlands – massive glaciers covering the land.

However, one small, unassuming dark brown butterfly managed to cling on during that bleak period in our geological and natural history. According to the guru of British lepidopterists, Jeremy Thomas, the Mountain Ringlet would have survived – even thrived – in the south of England, its numbers perhaps boosted by immigrants coming across the land bridge that still connected Britain to the European mainland at the time.

Today, the Mountain Ringlet is confined to a few parts of the Highlands and a small area of the English Lake District further south. This is one of several isolated populations of this montane butterfly, which is also found elsewhere in Europe's uplands, such as the Alps and Pyrenees. Our British race is smaller and drabber than its mainland European cousins, due to being isolated from one another for ten millennia. Today, it well deserves the title of Britain's toughest butterfly.

To see a Mountain Ringlet takes dedication, persistence and a lot of luck. The butterflies only emerge for two or three weeks, sometime from the middle of June onwards until perhaps the middle of July – slightly earlier or later in some years, depending on the prevailing weather conditions. To find them choose a sunny day – otherwise your chances of seeing one are virtually zero – and head up one of their known homes: Ben Lawers in Perthshire and Creag Meagaidh in Inverness-shire are two of the most reliable.

The craggy slopes of the Highlands are perhaps the last place you would expect to find a butterfly – but this is the stronghold of the Mountain Ringlet.

Mountain Ringlets usually live at altitudes of 450–730 m (1,500–2,400 ft) above sea level, although they can reach heights of over 900 m (3,000 ft), where no other butterfly is able to survive. The colonies live on the tops of mountain plateaux or in gullies running down the mountainside, where the grass is fairly short, or where there is damp ground alongside streams.

In cloudy or wet weather (the usual conditions on the high tops), the butterflies hide away in grassy tussocks, where they are almost impossible to find. When the sun does finally emerge, however, so do they – sometimes in their hundreds, even thousands – the males flying low over the ground in search of nectar-bearing alpine flowers such as Tormentil, Heath Bedstraw and Bilberry.

Your best chance of getting a good view is to look for an individual basking in the sunshine. The upperwings are a dark sepia brown, with a row of contrasting orange markings, each with a small black spot in the centre, along the trailing edge of each wing. Avoid confusion with the superficially similar (and much more common) Scotch Argus, which is also dark brown and orange, but is noticeably larger and has white dots in the patches on the wing.

Because each individual Mountain Ringlet may only live for a day or two, when it does emerge from its pupa this is a butterfly in a hurry. The males are far more active than the females, seeking out a mate with which they can breed. The females then lay their tiny eggs – up to 70 in a single day – on the blades of Mat Grass, a common species here.

Three weeks later, long after both their parents are dead, the caterpillars hatch and begin to feed voraciously on the blades of grass. By September they have reached almost full size, but instead of pupating they go into a long period of hibernation, emerging the following April or May to resume feeding. They finally pupate in late May or early June, emerging several weeks later as adult butterflies, and the cycle begins all over again.

Sadly the Mountain Ringlet may now be threatened as a British species, by the spectre of long-term climate change. Several known colonies at lower altitudes have disappeared in recent years, probably because as the climate warms up so the vegetation on the hillsides begins to alter. If climate change results in much higher temperatures, this specialised butterfly will simply have nowhere to go, and will become extinct in the Highlands and probably in the whole of Britain.

Chequered Skipper

Another Scottish speciality – indeed the only butterfly to occur nowhere else in Britain apart from the Highlands – is the Chequered Skipper. Of eight British skipper species, the Chequered Skipper is the most distinctive and arguably the most attractive – and not just because of its extreme rarity. As its name suggests, the Chequered Skipper has a dappled appearance, the dark brown wings being marked with distinctive creamy-orange blotches.

Today, this much sought-after butterfly is confined to the western Highlands, in parts of Argyllshire and west Inverness-shire. However, until the end of the Victorian era it could also be seen across much of southern England, and as recently as the 1970s an isolated population was found at several sites in the East Midlands. Today, the only evidence that it ever occurred south of the border is the Chequered Skipper gastropub in the village of Ashton, near Peterborough. By then, however, the species had also been discovered in Scotland – having been overlooked there until the start of the Second World War.

We don't usually think of butterflies as being territorial like birds – but this species certainly is. Males defend their little patch of ground fiercely against any rivals, perching in the sunshine with wings open before dashing out to intercept an intruding male. Females visit these territories to mate, then lay their eggs singly on the undersides of blades of grass.

Chequered Skipper caterpillars are the slowest to develop of any British butterfly, probably because they live in such a cool climate. They grow for more than three months before they begin to hibernate sometime in October. They emerge in the following spring, feed again and pupate before hatching out as adults. Unlike the Mountain Ringlet, which as its name suggests prefers upland habitats, Chequered Skippers are only found at low altitudes – usually below 200 m (660 ft) – on sunny slopes near broadleaved woodland, and generally close to water.

AUTUMN AROUND THE CORNER

By Midsummer's Day on 24 June, the summer soltice will have come and gone. From now on, although there is still the whole of July and August to come and temperatures will continue to rise, the amount of daylight each day gradually diminishes, a gentle but persistent reminder that autumn is on its way.

The sudden appearance of fungi such as this Fly Agaric in late summer is a sure signal that autumn is on its way.

Even before Midsummer's Day, a handful of summer visitors are already starting to head south. Most notable among these is the Cuckoo, males of which will, once they have mated, leave more or less immediately for their African wintering grounds. This means that a typical male Cuckoo may spend as little as two months – and certainly less than three – in the Highlands, raising the intriguing question as to whether we can even call it a British (or Scottish) bird. Yet although its stay here may be short, it has certainly made its presence felt. Even now, in Meadow Pipit nests from the Hebrides to Speyside, and the Flow Country to the Great Glen, young Cuckoos are growing day by day, these enormous babies keeping their foster parents on the go from dawn to dusk as they gather caterpillars for the hungry chick.

Signs of autumn are elsewhere, too. A Green Sandpiper from Scandinavia may turn up on the muddy edge of a loch, refuelling on its way south, also to spend the winter in Africa. On the coast, flocks of Knots from even further north – the High Arctic – arrive on the Ythan Estuary, still showing smudges of brick-red breeding plumage on their underparts. All across the Highlands, chicks are fledging, young mammals are leaving the safety of their nests and birdsong is coming to an end, as late spring merges inexorably into high summer, with autumn just over the horizon.

The next three months are a time of ease and plenty. With long hours of daylight, warm weather and plenty of food, most wild creatures can afford to relax, at least for a short while. Yet they must not ignore the fact that soon, when the chill winds of autumn begin to blow, they will have to prepare themselves to survive the long winter ahead.

Summer into Autumn

SUMMER SOLSTICE – THE OUTER LIMITS

As dawn breaks early on 21 June, so all across the northern hemisphere the longest day begins. To the north of the Scottish Highlands, at Stenness on the mainland of Orkney, a simple ceremony at sunrise marks the summer solstice, the day on which the sun reaches its zenith in the sky.

A group of people gather among the standing stones, which are probably the oldest in the British Isles, dating back more than 5,000 years to at least 3100 BC. They follow in a long and rather grisly tradition: the ancient inhabitants of these islands would carry bundles of human and animal bones to this special place, along with a live animal that they would then slaughter for a feast to mark the passing of the seasons.

Similar ceremonies are taking place to the west, at the Callanish stones on the Hebridean Isle of Lewis, and more than 1,100 km (almost 700 miles) to the south, at Stonehenge on Salisbury Plain. People gather on this special day, at these ancient Neolithic monuments, to try to find some spiritual or religious meaning in their lives; and many are able to do so. But for the wild creatures of the Highlands and Islands, the summer solstice has a far greater significance.

From now on, as the Earth gradually tilts on its axis so that the northern hemisphere moves away from the sun, the amount of daylight each day begins to decrease. It does so slowly and almost imperceptibly, so that neither the animals nor we notice it – at least at first. But decrease it does, so that by towards the end of September – the autumn equinox – the whole world experiences an equal share of a 12-hour day and 12-hour night. From then on, it will gradually become darker and darker until the low point of the winter solstice, just before Christmas.

A Spear Thistle is one of the classic plants of high summer in the Scottish Highlands, as indeed it is in the rest of Britain.

he standing stones of
allanish, on the Isle of
ewis, were put up by our
istant ancestors as a way
o mark the changing of
he seasons.

The changing position of the Earth in relation to the Sun is, of course, what gives us our seasons, and everywhere on these middle latitudes experiences the same significant and noticeable change. However, in and around the Scottish Highlands, especially on its northernmost fringes such as the Orkney archipelago, the change is made all the more noticeable because it is significantly further north than the rest of Britain.

For now, even though the amount of daylight gradually reduces day by day, the temperature continues to warm up. During the coming few months, from the end of June to at least the end of August and maybe beyond, it will mostly get warmer. Because of this – and the consequent availability of food – this is the easiest time for the fauna and flora of the Highlands, a time of abundance and plenty.

And yet, just over the horizon, there are reminders of the autumn and winter to come – six long months during which food will be scarce, the weather extreme and life tough for any creatures that choose to spend their whole lives here. These resident creatures must prepare for the lean times. They must use their instinct and experience to store food, build winter homes and ensure that they have the very best chance of surviving until the following spring.

Others will take a very different path. Knowing that the abundant insects on which they are feeding and that help them raise a family will soon disappear, they head away from the Highlands. Some travel short distances down to the coast or to southern Britain, where the weather is milder and the food supplies more reliable. Many, however, especially insect-eating birds such as warblers and flycatchers, have no choice but to head down to Africa, across Europe, the Mediterranean and the Sahara. They fly all the way across the Tropic of Cancer, the Equator and in some cases even the Tropic of Capricorn to end up in a place of plenty, where they spend our winter until they make the long journey home the following spring.

Meanwhile, here at the outer limits of the Scottish Highlands, in the wildest and most spectacular parts of Britain, this is the time when life is at its most plentiful and abundant. From the sea cliffs of Orkney to the beaches of the Isle of Mull, and the vast blanket bogs of the Flow Country to the mountains, forests and lochs of the Cairngorms and Strathspey, wild creatures are taking advantage of the long hours of daylight to grow, flourish and reproduce. Only by doing so will they ensure that their lineage continues down the generations, now and long into the future.

GO WITH THE FLOW

Visitors to the Scottish Highlands and Islands – especially those looking for the region's specialised wildlife – tend to concentrate at well-known hotspots: Speyside and the Cairngorms in the east, Islay, Mull and the Western Isles in the west, or further north to Orkney and Shetland. However, in doing so they often ignore what is arguably the most important of all the many superb areas for wildlife in the region: the Flow Country of Caithness and Sutherland.

Stretching over a vast expanse covering roughly 4,000 sq km (1,540 sq miles), and considerably larger than Suffolk, Kent or Cornwall, this bleak expanse of wet peatland and blanket bog does not immediately strike you as scenically beautiful – or even particularly rich in wildlife. Indeed, after experiencing the spectacular uplands to the south, or the rocky coasts and islands to the north and west, arriving here in the Flow Country can feel rather like an anticlimax.

A closer look appears to confirm this, as birds, mammals and even wild flowers seem very thin on the ground. From the air, all that stretches into the distance is mile after mile of grey-green, boggy terrain, criss-crossed by watercourses and relieved only by the occasional larger body of water. And yet, whatever these first impressions may lead you to believe, the Flow Country really is one of the prime wildlife habitats not just in Scotland, but in the whole of Britain and indeed Europe.

Walk across its boggy landscape for a few hours and although the number and variety of birds you see may not be very great, their quality stands out, be they waders such as the Golden Plover, Dunlin and Greenshank; waterbirds such as the Common Scoter and Black-throated Diver; or raptors such as the Hen Harrier and Merlin, all of which have their strongholds here.

Sphagnum moss is one of the characteristic plants of the boggy Flow Country in the far north of the Highlands.

he Sundew, a carnivorous
ant that prefers acid soils,
common and widespread
roughout the Flow Country.

There are also specialised plants, from the sphagnum moss that blankets the wetter areas, to the carnivorous butterworts and sundews, which compete with the birds for the abundant flies and midges that appear in their billions each summer, and plague unwary human visitors with their constant bites. Other, less annoying insects live here too: beneath the surface of the shallow, peaty waters are Great Diving Beetles, whose glossy black carapaces shine with iridescence when caught by the sun.

One hardy butterfly even manages to survive in this uncompromising habitat, so far north: the Large Heath. This unassuming pale brown and orange insect perches with its wings tightly closed on cotton grass and sedges; patiently waiting for the temperature to reach 14 °C (57 °F), at which point it takes to the wing and goes in search of nectar. Unlike for most other butterflies, the weather doesn't need to be sunny to enable it to fly – which, given the generally damp and cloudy conditions here, is just as well.

This precious habitat was almost destroyed during the early 1980s, when a scheme to plant trees there attracted high-profile investors keen to reap the benefits of a tax-free scheme. Unfortunately, though planting trees is usually good for the environment, covering this unique place with plantations of non-native trees, such as Sitka Spruce, was nothing short of an ecological disaster. Fortunately at the eleventh hour pressure from conservationists managed to halt the madcap scheme. Today much of the area is now an RSPB reserve – the biggest in the UK – where the wild creatures of the Flow Country are protected and can continue to thrive.

The Flow Country and forestry

Today, the unique landscape of the Flow Country is protected, but towards
the end of the 20th century it was very nearly destroyed. This was, ironically,
down to a government scheme to help wealthy people become even wealthier
by avoiding the payment of tax.

From the late 1970s onwards, accountants to wealthy city investors
and rich celebrities discovered that if their clients invested in a scheme to
plant trees, they would be eligible for massive tax rebates. For those then
paying the highest rates of tax this was a no-brainer, and many justified
it to themselves by the fact that planting trees is supposedly good for the
environment.

Unfortunately, these were the wrong trees in the wrong place: vast
stands of non-native conifers such as Norway and Sitka Spruce being
planted on precious expanses of blanket peat bog, one of the rarest and most
endangered habitats in the world. The planting of the trees was bad enough,
but the scheme also entailed draining large areas of land around the new
forests, causing even further environmental destruction. The future of the
Flow Country – and its very special wildlife – was in the balance.

Fortunately, at the eleventh hour environmentalists woke up to the
damage being caused, and persuaded the government to halt the scheme.
This, and widespread publicity castigating the celebrities and their advisors,
resulted in the forestry soon coming to an end. Of course, much damage
had already been done – and it has been estimated that it will take up to a
century to repair it, at a cost to the taxpayer of several million pounds.

Today, the central area of the Flow Country is under the management of
the RSPB, whose Forsinard reserve covers roughly 100 sq km (almost 40 sq
miles) of prime habitat. The RSPB is also campaigning for the Flow Country
to become a UNESCO World Heritage Site, something this quirky part of the
Highlands certainly deserves.

BRITAIN'S MOST BEAUTIFUL BIRD?

For many people, especially those lucky enough to have witnessed its extraordinary breeding displays, the Black-throated Diver would be near the top of any list of Britain's most beautiful birds. It may be, as its name suggests, monochrome in shade; it may live in places few of us ever have the privilege to visit; it may be shy and elusive. Yet it has a charisma and effortless beauty that once seen can never be forgotten.

The Black-throated is the rarer of our two breeding species of diver, with roughly 200 pairs compared with its cousin the Red-throated, which boasts well over 1,000 pairs. Red-throated Divers are easier to see, too, as they nest by roadside lochs in Shetland and Orkney, whereas Black-throated Divers prefer more remote and inaccessible sites such as the lochs of the Flow Country.

To find Black-throated Divers, you must be prepared to spend many hours trudging over these boggy landscapes, scanning any larger areas of water from a distance, and listening out for their characteristic call: a long, drawn-out wailing sound, which echoes around this otherwise often silent landscape. If you can hear the birds, it's essential to approach quietly and very carefully so as not to spook them. However, even from a safe distance, their effortless elegance will take your breath away.

Black-throated Divers are long, slender birds, sitting low in the water like surfaced submarines, as if ready to dive at any moment. During the breeding season they are slate-grey above, spangled with blocks of white markings on the upper back. They have a pale, dove-grey head, face and neck, black-and-white 'zebra stripes' down the sides of the neck, and a contrasting jet-black throat and pale belly. All this is set off by the bird's dagger-like bill and – in the only compromise to colour – deep blood-red eyes.

The remote lochs of the western and northern Highlands, like Loch Meadie, support very little life, though they are home to breeding Black-throated Divers.

With its strikingly
contrasting plumage and
streamlined shape, the
Black-throated Diver is one
of the most attractive of all
Scotland's birds.

The individual parts may sound dull – after all, the whole palette comprises mainly shades of black, white and grey – but the overall effect is simply stunning; all the more so, perhaps, because of the species' scarcity.

Black-throated Divers pair up for life – almost 30 years in some cases – but usually separate during the autumn and winter months, which they spend at sea, just off the coast. A particular couple renewed its pair bond earlier in the spring, coming to this remote patch of water and engaging in its courtship display. This involved a fascinating array of behaviours, including dipping the bills in the water, splashing and occasional diving beneath the surface, all of which helped cement the already strong bond between the male and female.

The male then built the nest with some help from the female, though to dignify this small patch of moss and rotting waterweed with the name 'nest' may be going too far. She then laid two dark, olive-coloured eggs covered with a few dark blotches and spots. The nest is usually just a few feet from the shore of the loch, as like all members of their family, Black-throated Divers have evolved to suit a life spent almost entirely on – or under – the water. Their feet are positioned towards the rear of the body; perfect for swimming and diving, but less than ideal for moving about on land.

Both the male and female took turns in incubating their clutch for almost a month, and when the young hatched they were, like most waterbirds, active and ready to swim within 24 hours of their birth. Now, in late June, they continue to be fed by their parents – on the small fish and aquatic invertebrates abundant in this loch. For this, perhaps the most crucial period of their lives, the young will stick close to the adults, as they will not fledge and gain their independence (and the ability to fly) until 8–9 weeks after hatching. However, if the parents leave them alone to hunt for food, the youngsters may sometimes become quite aggressive towards one another.

Watching Black-throated Divers is always a privilege. In such a remote and truly wild setting you always feel like a trespasser, which in some senses we humans are. For this land truly belongs to the birds: the wailing divers, Greenshank and Dunlin performing their songflights on still summer's evenings, and the sleek, streamlined Merlin shooting fast and low over the ground. He is on the lookout for unsuspecting Skylarks and Meadow Pipits, which he must catch to feed his own hungry brood of young, hidden in the heather somewhere nearby.

Significant Highlanders

JONATHAN WILLET ···
DRAGONFLY EXPERT AND WILDLIFE GUIDE

Most people come to the Highlands for the rare and spectacular creatures: Red Deer stags and Golden Eagles, Red Squirrels and Pine Martens, Capercaillies and Crested Tits. But some, like Jonathan Willet, prefer to focus on the miniature world of insects – in his case the dragonflies and damselflies. The Highlands may not have all that many different kinds, but it does boast some species found nowhere else in Britain, such as the stunning Azure Hawker, the tiny Northern Damselfly and the elusive Northern Emerald.

On a warm summer's day, Jonathan loves standing by a loch in the sun watching the insects' high-speed manoeuvres as their territorial and mating behaviour unfold in front of him. Part of his enjoyment comes from the sheer challenge of getting good views of these rapidly moving insects.

Jonathan's first experience of the Highlands came when he was just beginning to discover his passion for wildlife while working as a beater on the grouse moors of Perthshire. While studying for a Masters degree in ecology at Aberdeen University, he began to explore the region in greater depth, volunteered at Beinn Eighe National Nature Reserve and later began his first proper job at Aigas Field Centre near Beauly. He now works as a part-time biodiversity officer for Highland Council, spending the rest of his time doing dragonfly surveys and showing wildlife to visitors with his company, Red Kite Tours, now more than 10 years old.

For Jonathan, the history and culture of the Highlands is just as fascinating and important as the wildlife. He also enjoys the diversity of landscapes and habitats – for him unparalleled in Europe – and the consequent range of wildlife, which allows him to live and work in a place he loves.

When it comes to a favourite time of year, Jonathan takes inspiration from the old pagan culture of the Highlands, which divided the year into just two parts: the growing season and the dead season. Of the two, he not surprisingly chooses the growing season of spring and summer, when everything bursts into life, the days get longer and longer, and his beloved dragonflies and damselflies are on the wing.

His favourite place is a surprise: the often-overlooked Black Isle north-east of Inverness, with almost all the Highland habitats squeezed into a small area. However, as he notes, it is neither black, nor an island!

CITIES OF BIRDS

Back on the seabird island, off Scotland's north-west coast, it's been a good breeding season; a lot better than we might have imagined when that terrible storm hit the island earlier in the spring. Fortunately the weather improved, and a sunny and fairly dry May and June have allowed the seabirds to raise their chicks without fear of that terrible destruction from the Atlantic winds.

Fulmar (top) and Razorbill (bottom) are two of the many species of seabird that breed on the offshore islands around Scotland's coasts.

Seabird colonies are often reminiscent of human cities, more specifically tower blocks, in which different species choose to live at different levels, or as we might prefer to think of it, on different floors. Thus as you scan the cliff face from bottom to top, the lower floors are mainly populated by Razorbills and Kittiwakes, each pair having chosen a small nook or cranny in which the birds mark their tiny territory and lay their eggs. Razorbills do not make a nest as such – the female simply deposits her single egg at a suitable spot – where hopefully it will not be too close to the cliff edge, and in danger of falling off.

For Razorbills, like many auks and other seabirds, this egg is their only chance of reproduction. If it fails to hatch, or the chick is killed or dies, they will not normally breed again in the same year. Both male and female sit on the egg for roughly five weeks, after which the chick is constantly fed until it leaves the nest, usually when it is two or three weeks old.

Kittiwakes hedge their bets a little by building a more substantial nest out of seaweed, mud and grass, and laying two eggs – occasionally three – which both parents take turns to incubate for four or more weeks. Following this, the chicks may spend as long as five weeks in the nest, and may not fly until a few weeks after that.

Higher up the 'tower block', as the cliff ledges become narrower, we find the Guillemots. Like their cousins the Razorbills, these too lay a single egg; and those eggs that managed to survive the storm hatch out a week or two later. Both parents feed the chick, which has a major life event soon to come. When it is just 12 days old it will have to jump down into the sea in one of the most spectacular leaps of faith for any wild creature.

Meanwhile towards the top of the cliff, in the rough crevices and grassy patches where pinkish-purple clumps of thrift grow in abundance, we find a bird that, although it superficially resembles the Kittiwake, is not related to the gulls: the Fulmar. The name Fulmar means 'foul gull', because nesting birds will defend themselves and their young by spitting a disgusting sticky substance known as Fulmar oil onto any intruders, including, if you are not very careful, human ones. Fulmar oil is both foul smelling and incredibly hard to shift. It's inconvenient for us, if we get it on our clothing, but potentially fatal for any predator, such as a skua or Peregrine that ventures too close to the bird's nest.

Alongside the Fulmars, and indeed all across the grassy edges of the clifftops, we find the most sought-after and best loved of all our seabirds: the Puffin. Here in the penthouse suite Puffins nest in burrows: often the old homes of Rabbits, but sometimes dug by the birds themselves using their strong and powerful claws. Like most seabirds, Puffins lay a single egg. Most of the Puffins did so in mid-May, so now they have a hungry chick demanding to be fed. This presents a real difficulty for the Puffins, because to catch their staple diet of sand eels the adults must head out to sea.

When in their burrows, the Puffins are safe from the predators that gather around the edges of the seabird colony: the Great Black-backed Gulls, whose massive yellow bills can make short work of a smaller seabird; and the skuas, which are always on the lookout for a free meal. It is when the Puffins return from fishing out to sea that they are most at risk. Carrying a beakful of sand eels makes them front heavy, so they must flap their wings even more frantically than usual to stay aloft. Landing is a problem, too. Puffins have evolved a body shape to enable them to chase and catch fish under water, but when in the air or on land they appear clumsy and awkward.

As the male Puffin returns from his successful foraging trip, so a beady-eyed Great Black-backed Gull watches and waits. Just as the Puffin sweeps up the cliff face, using the updraught to lift him over the top, the gull pounces. He hits the Puffin square on, knocking him off balance, so that he drops some of his precious catch.

Now the battle is on: will the Puffin manage to reach his burrow before the gull catches him? The alternative is a quick but grisly death. The gull flies around in a tight circle as the Puffin makes his second approach, and targets the little bird once again. But this time the

Everyone's favourite seabird – the Puffin – also known as the 'sea parrot' because of its huge, colourful bill.

Puffin is determined not to be caught out. At the moment when the gull pounces, he manoeuvres in the air, twisting just out of the gull's reach. A moment later he reaches the entrance to his burrow, and safety.

A nearby Kittiwake is not so lucky. An Arctic Skua, with two growing chicks to feed, flies alongside the smaller gull, chasing and harassing him. He is not trying to kill the Kittiwake, simply to force him to regurgitate his catch of fish. Moments later, consumed by sheer panic, the Kittiwake gives up the fight and jettisons his precious cargo. The skua twists like a gymnast in mid-air, plummets down and grabs the bounty just before it hits the surface of the sea. Shaken but still alive, the Kittiwake returns to his nest on the cliff face empty-handed.

UNDERSEA WONDERS

Meanwhile, on the east coast of Scotland another hunt is going on. At Chanonry Point, on the northern side of the Moray Firth, east of Inverness, a crowd is gathering. The people watch and wait, full of tension, excitement and expectation, for what they are about to witness is one of the greatest wildlife spectacles of all – not just here in the Highlands, but anywhere in the British Isles.

They have come to see the resident pod of Bottlenose Dolphins doing what it does best: hunting salmon. As the tide goes out, so the salmon returning to the river start to gather offshore. To hunt them, the dolphins work as a team, concentrating their quarry into a tight shoal before chasing it down and grabbing it.

This is the most reliable place to watch these mighty cetaceans anywhere in Britain, and mighty they really are. Scotland's Bottlenose Dolphins are the biggest of their species in the world, some reaching a length of 4 m (13 ft), and weighing as much as 650 kg (1,400 lb). They can be told apart from other marine mammals such as the Harbour Porpoise by their larger size, long, curved dorsal fin and sociable habits – they are usually seen in pods of up to 50 individuals, whereas the porpoises are more often solitary or in pairs or smaller groups.

If you're really lucky, you will see the dolphins leaping right out of the water, then landing again with a huge splash. Look closely and you may also see smaller animals – newborn calves – swimming close alongside their mothers. Baby dolphins are usually born in late spring, summer or early autumn, and are dependent on their mother's milk for up to 20 months afterwards.

Dolphins are, as you would expect from such intelligent creatures, highly social animals. Living in a group enables them to develop a range of social skills, which in turn enables them to work with one another, and perform various duties such as 'baby-sitting' and cooperative hunting. They have few enemies, though in recent years they have become vulnerable to collisions with boats and possibly also to being disoriented by the use of military sonar, which messes up their communication systems and can cause them to become beached onshore.

Enthusiasts gather at Chanonry Point on the Moray Firth (top) to watch a regular pod of Bottlenose Dolphins (bottom).

KILLER WHALES

Further north, in the waters around Orkney, an even bigger creature is also searching for its prey. The Killer Whale – or Orca, as it is now often known – is the largest marine predator on the planet. A male can reach a length of almost 10 m (more than 30 ft), and tip the scales at 5 tonnes – roughly seven times the weight of the largest Bottlenose Dolphin.

Seeing an Killer Whale in British waters is never easy or predictable, but a visit to the seas around Orkney during the middle of summer gives you as good a chance as any. This mighty animal is simply unmistakable: a huge, bulbous, black head emerges from the water, revealing a white patch behind the eye and another, larger white area beneath its mouth. However, often the first sign that a pod of Killer Whales is cruising along in the shallow waters around the islands is the appearance of a long, sickle-shaped object protruding momentarily above the surface of the waves: the animal's huge dorsal fin.

Like Bottlenose Dolphins, Killer Whales are sociable creatures, usually living in a pod of 15–20 individuals, though further out into the North Sea groups of several hundred have been seen. The most widespread marine mammal on the planet, Killer Whales hunt in packs, mobilising themselves tactically to corner their prey so that they have an easier task in catching it. Rip tides, when water rushes rapidly away from the shore, are good places to look for them, as this also concentrates the fish into a single area.

By midsummer the calves (mostly born the previous autumn or winter) are 6–9 months old. As in the case of Bottlenose Dolphins, the youngsters are dependent on their mothers for both milk and protection, though as the largest and most fearsome predator in the seas, the Killer Whale has no real enemies.

On a summer's evening off the Orkney island of Hoy, a pod of Killer Whales drifts close inshore. They hunted earlier in the day, so for now there is no urgency about them. From time to time they float on the surface of the calm blue sea, their heads bobbing above the water as they appear to survey the scene. Then, without warning, they dive and swim strongly out to sea, to renew their mysterious lives.

The Orca – or Killer Whale – is the mightiest of all marine predators, and can be seen in small numbers off Scotland's coasts, especially in midsummer and early autumn.

SEAL CITY

Elsewhere on Orkney, on the tiny island of Eynhallow, another marine mammal has come ashore to breed. Up to 900 Common (or Harbour) Seals visit here every summer, squeezing onto an island less than a third of a square mile (75 ha) in area. Once they would have shared this place with a score of hardy human inhabitants, but the people who used to live here finally left the island more than 150 years ago. Today, seabirds are the most abundant creatures found here, with both species of skua (Arctic and Great), Fulmar, Puffin, Arctic Terns and a few Black Guillemots (known locally as 'tysties') all nesting.

Each June, the Common Seals arrive here en masse, hauling themselves out on the sandy beaches beneath the 20 m (65 ft) high cliffs. Despite their name, they are the rarer of our two resident seal species, with roughly 40,000–50,000 individuals in the British Isles, compared with about 200,000 Atlantic Grey Seals. However, globally they are far more common, with as many as six million found throughout the cool temperate latitudes of the northern hemisphere from Alaska and Canada in the west, across northern Europe, to Russia and Japan in the east. In Scotland, Common Seals can be seen around all the coasts.

If you spot a lone seal it may not always be easy to identify. Ignore the colour, as both Common and Grey Seals are very variable in shade. Instead look at the head and face: a Grey Seal has a domed snout, giving it a rather haughty appearance, whereas a Common Seal is more dog-like, with a friendlier expression. It is also smaller than a Grey: a typical Common Seal weighs about 100 kg (220 lb), compared with up to 440 kg (970 lb) for a big Grey Seal.

Common Seals like this one are sometimes hard to tell apart from their cousin the Grey Seal. Look out for their dog-like appearance.

Unlike Grey Seals (bottom), which give birth in late autumn, Common Seals (top) do so in summer, in colonies on beaches around Scotland's coasts.

So on a fine, light evening towards the end of June, the Common Seals come ashore on Eynhallow. The males and females actually mated almost a year ago, last July, but like several species of mammal they are able to delay implanting the fertilised egg so that the pup is born at the right time of year.

For the next two or three weeks the beaches of Eynhallow resound to the grunts and groans of female Common Seals giving birth. They do so in the area below the high-tide mark, and once the single pup is born it is able to swim and dive almost immediately – unlike Grey Seal pups, which stay on land for several weeks before venturing into the sea. The mother is therefore able to feed during the suckling period – again, unlike the female Grey Seal.

Seal milk is one of the most concentrated and nutritious of all mammal milks – crucial if the pup is to reach its desired weight within the period of a month or so when the mother is feeding it. Once it has weaned, sometime in early August, it will head out to sea. Sadly, Common Seal pups are very vulnerable in their first few months of life. They can become caught in fishing nets and, unable to free themselves, drown; they may be hit by a passing boat; or they may simply not find enough food and eventually starve to death.

On a lighter note, seals have – as we might expect from such an endearing animal – become deeply rooted in our folklore and popular culture. The best-known story is that of the 'selkie' – a mythical creature supposed to be half-seal, half-human – which is well known around the coasts of the Highlands and Islands. The story goes that once the selkie leaves the sea it sheds its skin on the shore and becomes human. But when it tries to return, if the skin has been lost or stolen the selkie must remain on land, trapped as a human being forever.

Like many 'shape-shifting' myths, that of the selkie tells us more about ourselves than about the seals. Over the centuries the selkie myth has been celebrated and perpetuated in songs, poems, ballads and stories, perhaps suggesting that as humans we will always seek out mystery, especially if it is connected with the sea.

SUMMER IN THE FORESTS

After the burst of spring birdsong, the Caledonian pine forests are once again quiet. July is a month of plenty here, as it is across all of the Highlands, when long summer days and an abundance of food make life easy – for the moment, at least. But as at any time of year, there are still new creatures to be seen – as long as you know where to look. One of these creatures occurs along the forest rides – it's a dark, velvet-brown butterfly sporting a row of orange blotches along the edges of its wings, which flutters purposefully along.

It is a Scotch Argus, one of Scotland's most common summer butterflies, which despite its name does just about edge its range into England – with outlying colonies in the Lake District. Here in the Highlands it is on the wing from the last week of July into the first week of September – a brief but hopefully warm and sunny period during which it must mate, and the female lay her eggs on clumps of Purple Moor-grass.

The male Scotch Argus is constantly on the wing, hardly ever coming to rest as it flies low over the surface of the Purple Moor-grass in search of a female. If you do get a closer look, you'll notice the false 'eyes' in the centre of each orange blotch: dark patches with a tiny white spot in the centre, which will fool a predatory bird into pecking at the wing-tip rather than the body, and thus allow the insect to escape – albeit often with a ragged, torn wing.

Mature Scots Pines – sometimes referred to as 'Granny' pines – are a good indicator of native woodland and in late summer the understory of flowering heather and bilberries provides cover and food for many species of birds, mammals and invertebrates.

The Scotch Argus, as its name suggests, is a classic Highland butterfly, on the wing in late summer.

Although its stronghold is in the Scottish Highlands, the Scotch Argus is not usually found at altitudes above 500 m (1,640 ft) – a habitat it leaves to the much scarcer Mountain Ringlet. Instead it prefers woodland clearings, the edges of sheltered boggy areas and even roadside verges – so long as there is long grass. Strangely, given that it lives in some of the wettest places of Britain, it is very dependent on sunshine, rarely flying when the sun is not out, although it will take to the wing on overcast days as long as the air temperature is warm enough.

As the male Scotch Argus heads off to search for a mate, so the high-pitched sound in the conifer canopy above reveals the presence of a small flock of Crested Tits – including the surviving members of the brood we saw earlier in the year. Having laid their eggs in April, the young hatched towards the end of that month, and fledged and left the safety of their nest in the rotten birch stump in mid-May.

Now, a couple of months later, they have become independent of their parents, but because they are still living in the area where they hatched they may still come across one another as they search through the pine needles for food. Two other tiny birds may accompany them: Goldcrests and Coal Tits, both of which seek safety in numbers after breeding.

All three species feed constantly and actively, moving from branch to branch and searching the underside of the foliage for tiny insects. They will remain in the same area for the rest of the summer, and also during the autumn and winter, before – if they manage to survive (and most do not) – pairing up to breed next spring.

They call almost continually to stay in touch with their fellow feeders. All three make very high-pitched sounds, inaudible to some human ears, especially as our ability to hear these very high frequencies diminishes with age. Listen out for a thin, 'see-see-see' made by the Coal Tit; the even higher-pitched 'tsee' of the Goldcrest, and the more distinctive trill of the Crested Tit – a rhythmic, repetitive sound that once learnt is the best way to locate this elusive species.

The real Loch Ness Monster

Loch Ness – the largest loch in the Highlands – is famous the world over as the supposed home of the Loch Ness Monster. Yet although this mythical creature has captured our imagination for years, another very real monster lurks in the watery depths.

The ferox trout is a fish that lives up to its name – the Latin word ferox means fierce, or ferocious. Ferox trout begin life as ordinary Brown Trout, feeding happily on tiny insects. However, as they grow and develop, they turn nasty. They change their diet to fish, and even on occasions turn cannibal to consume smaller members of their own species. They can grow much bigger than 'normal' Brown Trout, reaching a length of 80 cm (31 in).

Ferox trout evolved in the lochs of the Scottish Highlands for two reasons. First, they became reproductively isolated from other populations of Brown Trout; then, they were forced to find alternative food sources due to a shortage of food in these vast water bodies. The lochs of the Highlands are oligotrophic – meaning that they have very low levels of nutrients – as opposed to the eutrophic, nutrient-rich lakes of lowland Britain. This is a result of the Highlands' geology: when rainwater runs over rocks it usually leaches out some of the nutrients held within, but the ancient granite bedrock of the Scottish Highlands is so hard that few nutrients ever reach the water.

As a result, aquatic plants grow either very slowly or not at all, which means that the plethora of aquatic insects and other invertebrates found in eutrophic lakes fails to materialise. No plants or insects means no food for the trout – hence their carnivorous tendencies.

Incidentally, for the same reasons that the ferox trout has had to turn into a top predator – the lack of nutrients resulting in there being not much to eat in the Highland lochs – the Loch Ness Monster could not possibly exist, as no creature of this massive size could ever manage to survive here.

WATERWORLDS

The pine forests of the Highlands are not, as you might imagine, an unbroken stretch of continuous woodland. Instead they are broken up with areas of open ground – bog and moorland – and of course lochs and lochans. In high summer it is these water bodies that are home to some of the area's most fascinating and beautiful creatures.

Glen Affric is, quite rightly, hailed as a beauty spot; indeed, it is often said to be the most beautiful of all of Scotland's many glens. West of the charming little town of Beauly, it attracts thousands of visitors each year: hikers and climbers, anglers and birders, mountain bikers and photographers. They mostly come here to admire the amazing scenery. However, one small but select group of visitors spends most of its time looking down, not up. These people wade into the edge of the sedge-fringed Coire Loch rather than trekking across the hills. They search not for easily seen birds or deer, but for some of the Highlands' most special insects: the dragonflies and their smaller cousins, the damselflies (often known simply as 'dragons and damsels').

Dragonflies are creatures of sunshine and warmth, perhaps more associated with the summer than any other group of insects. They emerge from April to October, but for most species – especially those found here in the Highlands – the peak time to look for them are the months of June, July and August.

Britain boasts roughly 40 resident species of dragonfly and damselfly, but far fewer than this are found in Scotland, with just 16 species (five damselflies and 11 dragonflies) regularly seen in the Highlands themselves. These include several species that are common and widespread throughout much of Britain, such as Common Blue and Emerald Damselflies, the Four-spotted Chaser, and the inappropriately named Southern Hawker.

Small lochs, such as this one at Glen Affric, are home to some of Britain's scarcest and most sought-after dragonflies and damselflies.

ae Northern Emerald is
ne of the toughest of
ne world's dragonflies,
referring cool climates
uch as that of the
cottish Highlands.

However, the majority of the dragons and damsels found in the Highlands are either scarce in the rest of Britain, such as the Common Hawker, the Downy and Brilliant Emeralds, and the huge yellow-and-black Golden-ringed Dragonfly; or are not found south of the border at all. It is the latter group of four species – the Northern Damselfly, Northern Emerald, Azure Hawker and Highland Darter – together with the very localised White-faced Darter, that attract visitors wanting to fulfil their ambition of seeing every British dragon and damsel in the wild.

First stop on this quest is the RSPB's Loch Garten reserve in Speyside, where the pools near the visitor centre are home to the delicate, greenish-blue Northern Damselfly and the handsome White-faced Darter, as well as the occasional Northern Emerald. Some people continue north to Glen Affric, or further on to the Bridge of Grudie by Loch Maree, both of which are noted hotspots for these sought-after species.

Searching for Highland dragonflies – even in midsummer – can be a frustrating affair, as overcast, rainy or windy days all make it far harder to find them. That perhaps explains why Scottish dragonfly experts have turned to checking beneath the surface of the water for both dragonfly larvae and what are called 'exuviae' – the outer casing left behind when an adult dragonfly or damselfly finally emerges from its long period of underwater development.

However, if the sun does come out, then so do the dragons and damsels: delicate Common Blue Damselflies, alternately banded with black and bright blue, together with the slightly longer Emerald Damselflies, which perch with their wings held out at a 45-degree angle to their body, unlike other damselflies, which fold their wings straight back along the abdomen.

Black Darters – the mature males jet-black in colour, the young males and females a pale yellow with black, go-faster stripes – swarm low over the boggy area by the side of the loch. Highland Darters, the darker version of the Common Darter, and perhaps simply a distinctive race of that widespread species, are also abundant here.

Then a flash of green catches your eye as a larger, longer dragonfly zooms past. This is where your powers of identification are really challenged, for all three British species of emerald dragonfly can be found here. They can only be told apart by subtle differences in their shape and, to the expert eye, their habits.

Downy Emeralds fly fast and low, and can be very territorial, attacking any intruders into their airspace. Brilliant Emeralds prefer shadier spots, often flying under overhanging trees, which Downy Emeralds rarely do. They also have a straighter abdomen, with a less pinched 'waist' than their cousins.

The third member of this metallic-green trio is the Northern Emerald which, as its name suggests, lives in the upper latitudes of Europe and Asia, from Ireland to Japan. Here in Britain it can only be seen in the Scottish Highlands, where it prefers peat bogs, mainly at low altitudes. As well as patrolling over the surface of the loch, it also rises up to feed on small insects along the tops of the surrounding trees, where it can be frustratingly too distant to distinguish from its cousins.

However, the dragonfly most visitors have come to see is not usually seen flying over the water, but is more likely to be found perched on a dead tree or rock alongside the path around the loch. This is the Azure Hawker, one of the toughest insects on the planet. Found right across the boreal regions of Scandinavia and Siberia, it is one of the few dragonflies regularly sighted north of the Arctic Circle.

In Britain the Azure Hawker is confined to Scotland, with the vast majority in the Highlands apart from a small, outlying population in Galloway in the Scottish Borders. Look out for a large, slender dragonfly (typical of all hawkers), with pale blue and brown markings. But beware – the Azure closely resembles the larger Common Hawker. The main difference between them is that the male Common Hawker appears browner and has yellow markings, whereas the Azure Hawker, as its name suggests, is predominantly blue.

All these dragonflies and damselflies are gamblers: they have evolved to live in what to some might be seen as a hostile place where, even at the height of summer, the weather can be cool and wet. However, all they need are a few sunny days during which they can breed and the females lay their eggs. Most of their life cycle goes on beneath the waters of the loch, where the nymph spends years developing before it finally emerges as an adult.

Seen up close, this emerald damselfly reveals its extraordinary compound eyes, which enable it to react to movement in an instant.

The Inglorious Twelfth?

A date that features prominently in the Highland calendar is 12 August, which marks the start of the grouse-shooting season. For some, the 'Glorious Twelfth' allows shooters to pit their wits against one of the fastest-flying birds of all. For others this is an anachronism during which ludicrously rich people pay a small fortune to take potshots at a wild bird.

The Red Grouse used to be considered our only endemic grouse species (see p. 38), but is now known to be simply a race (albeit a very distinctive one) of the widespread Willow Grouse, which can be found right across the northern hemisphere. Nevertheless, it remains a precious part of our natural heritage, and is also arguably Britain's most controversial bird.

The arguments for grouse shooting are that it helps to preserve this distinctive British race, which otherwise might die out; and that maintaining its specialised moorland habitat helps other species such as the Dunlin, Golden Plover and Merlin. Grouse shooters also point to the benefits their sport brings to the rural economy in the Highlands by providing jobs.

Those against grouse shooting have equally powerful arguments: that most of the money generated goes into the pockets of wealthy landowners, who are also heavily subsidised by the taxpayer in the form of farming subsidies; and that the maintenance of moors by burning releases carbon into the atmosphere, causes flooding and benefits only a small proportion of Britain's wildlife at the expense of many other species.

However, their strongest argument against grouse shooting is a legal and moral one: that the gamekeepers on grouse moors, with the overt or tacit support of the landowners, deliberately target the Hen Harrier, a bird of prey known to predate on grouse chicks. Shooting or trapping any bird of prey, including the Hen Harrier, is illegal, yet because there are rarely witnesses to these crimes, the criminals usually go unpunished.

ON THE BEACH

As autumn takes a grip on the Highlands and Islands, so the wind whips up the sea, and white-crested waves come crashing down on the beaches around the coasts. Any summer holidaymakers are by now long gone and the beaches are deserted, apart from the odd gull surfing the wind, feathers ruffled by the strengthening autumn gale as it battles along the shoreline.

But on a select few coasts – from Copinsay in the north, via the Monach Isles in the west, to the Moray Firth in the east – there is plenty of noise, bustle and activity. For here are the breeding colonies of Scotland's largest resident mammal, the Atlantic Grey Seal. Now, as late-autumn storms and gales lash the coastlines around the Highlands, this huge and charismatic mammal is about to enter the most critical period in its life cycle. The female seals are preparing to go into labour – and they do so at a time when the worst of the weather is about to strike.

Way out in the Atlantic, hundreds of miles to the west of Scotland, a storm is brewing. A deepening trough of low pressure, surrounded by swirling anti-clockwise winds, is gaining strength and momentum. Soon it will be carried rapidly eastwards across the ocean, and crash into our shores in what meteorologists call a 'weather bomb'.

For the human population of the Highlands and Islands this is bad enough: people are battening down the hatches and preparing for what the weather forecasters say will be one of the strongest storms ever to hit these exposed coasts. But for the mother Grey Seal on the island of Copinsay, the coming storm is far more serious, for she is about to give birth to her single pup; a pup that must, in its first few days of life, survive this terrible weather event. At the moment, though, the skies are clear, there is only a light breeze blowing across the rocky beach and the female lies calmly on the shoreline, unaware of the danger now just hours away.

Grey Seals breed at a number of rocky beaches around the northern and western coasts of the Highlands, and particularly in the northern isles of Orkney and Shetland.

ike any coastal animal, Grey
eals are very vulnerable to
utumn and winter storms.

VERLEAF *After giving birth,
emale Grey Seals mate with
he larger, stronger males
efore heading back to sea.*

Until yesterday she was fishing for food offshore, eager to build up her energy and fat reserves, for once she has given birth she will not eat again for the next three weeks. Instead she will live on her reserves of stored fat, until her pup no longer depends on her for food. Now, however, she hauls herself up the beach and her labour finally begins. An hour or so later she gives birth to her offspring, which is about the size and weight of a full-grown Cocker Spaniel. Unlike his mother, who has a blotchy grey coat, the pup is covered in a thick layer of soft white fur.

This unusual colouring is thought to be a hangover from the last ice age, when having a white coat would have given the pups an evolutionary advantage, enabling them to hide on beaches covered with snow and ice. Why this has survived into the present day is a mystery; it certainly makes newborn Grey Seal pups stand out against the grey rocks of their birthplace. Maybe, given the lack of predators, this doesn't really matter.

Like most baby mammals, as soon as the pup has been born he starts to suckle from his mother. The milk he feeds on is one of the richest and most nutritious of any mammal, with up to 60 per cent fat and plenty of protein; essential if the pup is going to survive the coming winter. Before he gets that far, however, he has

a more urgent problem to face – the growing storm. During the time that he has been feeding so hungrily, the winds have been strengthening, and the first flurries of rain and sleet are peppering the beach. Out to sea the swell is getting higher and higher, and now huge waves are crashing over the beach, pushing the rising water closer and closer to the mother and pup.

The mother now faces a difficult choice. Her first instinct is to keep her pup where he is, for she is still weak from the efforts of labour, and he needs to feed. But as the storm gets stronger and stronger, another instinct kicks in; the need to protect her pup at all costs. She pulls away from him as he feeds, then nudges him from the rear with her snout. At first he does not respond, trying in vain to suckle once again. She is persistent and he finally gets the message, reluctantly moving up the beach, propelling himself forwards with his flippers. His retreat comes not a moment too soon, for the tide is rising too, and due to this, combined with the storm surge created by wind and waves, the once wide and empty beach is now rapidly disappearing underwater.

As the mother and pup make their painfully slow progress, crawling higher and higher up the beach towards safety, the water laps at their tails. Finally, after what seems like hours they reach the top of the beach,

where rock and sand give way to the start of a grassy field. Exhausted by his efforts so soon after being born, the pup stops for a rest and the female looks round to see a watery maelstrom where the beach used to be.

Other pups have not been so fortunate. Perhaps they were too weak to move, or their younger and less experienced mothers did not realise the danger they were in. As the winds began to batter the shoreline, they were caught by the rising waves and swept helplessly out to sea to die. In a day or two, perhaps, their lifeless bodies will be washed up on the same shore where they were born, while others will sink to the bottom of the sea, all sad casualties of the storm.

The Atlantic Grey Seal

Of all Britain's resident mammals, apart from the various whales and dolphins that visit the seas around our coasts, the largest is the Atlantic Grey Seal. Males tip the scales at up to 440 kg (970 lb), and can reach a length of 2.5 m (8 ft). Although the females are considerably smaller they are still formidable beasts, weighing an average of 155 kg (340 lb) and 1.8 m (6 ft) long. Male Grey Seals are considerably larger than the biggest terrestrial mammal in Scotland, the Red Deer, which rarely weighs more than 220 kg (480 lb).

Grey Seals are one of two species of seal breeding in Scotland, the other being the smaller Common (or Harbour) Seal. The two species can be told apart not by their colour – Common Seals can appear grey as well – but by the shapes of their muzzles. Grey Seals have a 'Roman nose', which gives them a rather haughty, horse-like appearance – indeed, an alternative name for the species is Horsehead Seal. Common Seals look much friendlier, rather like large dogs.

Close to half the world population of Grey Seals lives around our coasts – more than 200,000 animals in all, the vast majority of which are found in Scotland. Yet just a century ago the species was highly endangered, with just a few hundred individuals found in the whole of Britain.

The Grey Seal's comeback was largely due to a pioneering piece of legislation, the Grey Seals Protection Act, which was passed by parliament on the eve of the First World War in 1914. This Act – which restricted the killing of seals during the critical late-autumn breeding season – was a great success; indeed, so much so that fishermen continue to call for the seals to be culled because they take fish stocks. For now at least, however, the species continues to enjoy full legal protection, and is thriving.

BACK TO SEA

Even having survived the terrors of the storm, our seal pup may still struggle to survive. From now on his mother needs to feed him five or six times a day, until he has more than doubled his birth weight to over 30 kg (65 lb). If she runs out of milk before the pup is three weeks old, he will starve to death.

By the time he reaches that stage in his life, he looks completely different. The white fur has been replaced with a coat of mottled greyish-brown, similar to that of his mother. More importantly, unlike the fur it replaced this new coat is also waterproof. It needs to be, for soon the mother will abandon her offspring, leaving him to fend for himself. When this happens, at first the pup seems bemused by the sudden change in his circumstances. He sits forlornly at the top of the beach, presumably waiting for his mother to return. As hours – then days – pass, it finally dawns on the hungry pup that this is never going to happen. He faces a simple choice: stay put and starve to death, or head for the sea.

This is perhaps the most dangerous moment in the little animal's life. Having never swum before, he relies purely on instinct – and that tells him to get as far offshore as quickly as possible, before those big waves drive him back onto the jagged rocks. Even so, it takes two or three failed attempts before he finally manages to swim out past the waves, and finds himself in what will become his home for the next few weeks, months and years: the sea.

Meanwhile, you might expect that the exhausted and starving mother seal would also head back out to sea to feed, after her prolonged period of self-inflicted starvation. There is one last thing she needs to do, however, and that is mate. When she left her pup for that last time, she crawled slowly across the rocks to the next beach, from where strange sounds were coming – the sounds of fighting Grey Seal males.

Savage storms often batter the coasts of Scotland during the late autumn and winter months, sometimes creating mounds of sea foam.

Grey Seal pups have a white fur coat from birth until a few weeks afterwards, when they moult into their adult garb and brave the high seas for the very first time in their short but eventful lives.

For the past three weeks, while the female has been busy tending to her pup, the males have had other things on their minds. Like the Red Deer whose rut fills the autumn air with bellows and grunts, they too have been fighting. This is a very serious fight indeed: the long, violent and sometimes bloody contest to decide which male will get the chance to mate with the most females. Again, like the Red Deer rut, it looks both gruesome and rather pointless. However, nothing could be further from the truth. This is the best way to ensure that the females mate with the biggest, strongest and fittest males, thus passing the genes for survival onto their offspring.

The males have waited a long time for this. A decade has passed since they first left the safety of the beach as tiny pups, and started to explore their new marine home. For ten long years they have fed, hauled out to rest and fed again, gradually building up their strength until now, at last, they are ready to enter the fray. They need to be as strong and fit as possible, for these fights are brutal and bloody, with the seal's tough skin often broken by the teeth of a rival.

Even when they have won the right to mate with the patient, watching females, the violence isn't over. Seal mating is not a pretty sight, for having not fed for at least three weeks, and passed on much of her energy reserves to her offspring, the female is thin and weak, no match for the heavy, testosterone-fuelled male. He mounts her roughly and does the deed, after which he collapses exhausted, before finally leaving the battleground and returning to the sea.

She is pregnant again, but because her gestation period is almost the same as that of humans – roughly nine months – she now needs to delay implanting the fertilised egg inside her womb, so that she gives birth at the same time next year. Thus the complex cycle of seal life continues. Once in a while, however, this cycle of life is disrupted by what may at first appear to be a truly horrific event: infanticide. The killing of young mammals by adult males is more common than we might imagine. Male Lions invariably kill the offspring of their rivals when they take over a pride, which makes sound evolutionary sense – why would you invest precious time and energy raising cubs that are not your own?

In marine mammals this phenomenon is less well documented, but that may simply be because it is not so easy to observe. We do know that several species of seal and sea lions kill young pups – either squashing them by accident during mating, or deliberately. Male Grey Seals have been observed to shake, bite and savage pups, and drag them into the water, where they drown. From time to time the killing even leads to cannibalism, as the victorious male consumes his unfortunate victim.

PETER CUNNINGHAM ··· FISH BIOLOGIST

Born in Edinburgh, Peter has been living in Wester Ross since 2001, working as a biologist for the Wester Ross Fisheries Trust. Like many conservationists, he splits his time between the office and the outdoors, aiming to maintain healthy wild fish populations for the benefit of anglers and wildlife.

This is the culmination of a childhood dream; he started fishing as a child, when his dad showed him how to catch trout on the island of Jura. But he also loves the diversity of wildlife in Wester Ross, and the variety of habitats in such a small area: mountaintops, open moorland, oak, birch and Scots Pine woods, rivers, lochs and lochans, and some of the most diverse marine habitats anywhere in the UK.

Peter is well aware of problems: many habitats have been degraded, and he is proud to be part of the mission to restore places for wildlife on land and at sea. On land, he feels there are too many Red Deer, which degrade the soils, while at sea fish farms are a problem, as they allow sea lice to proliferate.

Peter likes having something new to enjoy at every season of the year. Each spring he sets himself a challenge to find 100 species of vertebrate (birds, mammals, amphibians and fish) around Gairloch, his favourite part of the Highlands. There's a catch – he must do it on foot!

In summer he heads off in his kayak to fish for mackerel or put out a creel for crabs and lobsters – and may encounter Minke Whales and Basking Sharks. He's less keen on two smaller creatures, both abundant during the Highland summer: midges and clegs. In autumn he snorkels in the sea around Wester Ross, and he sees Sea Trout as they head up the burns to spawn, and watches salmon as they leap upriver.

As someone who has devoted his working life to trout, Peter's favourite creature is not in question. He admires its variety, from non-migratory Brown Trout that live in lochs above waterfalls, to migratory Sea Trout found around the coast, which represent a crucial lifeline between the sea and headwater streams.

Peter advises visitors to get up early and look for wildlife for themselves, rather than always relying on guides and guidebooks. He is keen to get more youngsters out and about in the Highlands – including his own nieces and nephews.

LEAP OF FAITH

Fortunately, the majority of Grey Seal pups escape such a grisly fate, and the lucky ones survive long enough to reach adulthood. That's not, however, the case for another species that also breeds at this time of year: the Atlantic Salmon. Individual salmon really do have the odds stacked against them at almost every stage of their lives. Indeed, it sometimes seems a miracle that any manage to survive at all. They do, though, and as autumn reaches its peak, so does one of the greatest events of the Highland wildlife calendar: the leaping of the Atlantic Salmon as they return to their riverine birthplace to breed.

Standing on the rather rickety suspension bridge over Rogie Falls, on the Black Water north-west of Inverness, the rushing water looks dark, cold and uninviting – which indeed it is. The air is cold, too, so it makes sense to wrap up warm, for you may be in for a long wait. At first, nothing seems to be happening, then a whirr of wings signals a Dipper heading downstream, followed soon afterwards by the thin, metallic, high-pitched call of a Grey Wagtail from somewhere out of sight.

Then, in the pool below the falls, something breaks the surface: a silvery glint of fish-scales, which rapidly retreats back into the dark water. Another flash, then another, then the unforgettable sight of an adult male salmon breaking through the surface of the river like a guided missile, leaving the water completely. Drops fall off the surface of his skin and back down into the blackness of the pool, as he flies through the air. However, momentum and strength will only take him so far; gravity too has a say, and he slows, and slows, until he finally crashes back into the water with a mighty splash. The salmon run has begun.

Few sights in the Highlands are more awe-inspiring and spectacular than an Atlantic Salmon leaping upriver to breed.

Over the course of the next few days, dozens of Atlantic Salmon will attempt to get up and over the waterfall. Most will fail and drop exhausted back into the lower reaches of the river, their life's task unfulfilled. Those that do manage to get over the falls will have leapt about 4 m (13 ft) into the air, appearing to defy gravity as they do so. Others will use the 'salmon ladder' thoughtfully installed at the side of the falls by conservationists. This allows the fish to get over the falls in a number of easier stages; nevertheless, many seem to prefer the challenge of making death-defying leaps over the falls themselves.

Sadly there are fewer Atlantic Salmon on this and many other Highland rivers than there used to be. This decline is down to a whole range of problems in both rivers and the open sea, from pollution to the damaging effect of salmon farms, as well as changes in habitat caused by climate change. Efforts are being made to help the Atlantic Salmon, which is a keystone species of our rivers, as it is both eaten by, and in turn preys on, a wide range of other river creatures.

This salmon ladder at Rogie Falls has been designed to enable the returning fish to reach their birthplace more easily.

The Atlantic Salmon life cycle

No other Highland creature has quite such a complex life cycle as the 'king of fish' – the Atlantic Salmon – one of the very few species that can happily live in both fresh and salt water.

The Atlantic Salmon's life begins – and often ends – in a pool towards the top of a Highland river such as the Spey or Dee. The fish emerge in spring out of a tiny egg – one of several thousand laid by the female – and at hatching are about 2 cm (less than 1 in) long, and are called alevins. These tiny fish hide away in the gravel on the riverbed for the first few weeks of their life, feeding on a yolk sac. Once this food supply has been exhausted, after about 4–6 weeks, they emerge, at which point they are known as fry.

During the following year they feed voraciously and grow rapidly, developing into the next stage, called parr. These stay in the area where they were born for between six months and three years, though because of predators such as Herons and Otters very few actually survive that long – perhaps one in ten overall. Then they change again, losing their striped camouflage and developing a silvery appearance – at this stage they are called smolts – to be ready to head out to sea. By this time their body chemistry has undergone the crucial changes that allow them to live in salt water.

Salmon then spend up to six years out in the open ocean, where they grow and develop into full adults. Only then does some mysterious force impel them to return all the way to their birthplace, fighting their way upstream using their incredible sense of smell and built-in navigation system. Once back, they mate and the female lays thousands of eggs. As she does so the male approaches and deposits his sperm to fertilise the eggs; then both usually die exhausted, their life's work done.

ARRIVALS FROM THE NORTH

The skies are clear, the frost is crisp on the ground and a ringing sound fills the air. As dusk begins to fall over the crystal-clear waters of the Loch of Strathbeg, on the Aberdeenshire coast, the geese are coming in to roost. Tens of thousands of Pink-footed Geese throng the skies, their calls increasing in volume and intensity as they approach their resting place. As they do so, they seem to hang in the air for a moment of two, before folding their wings and plummeting rapidly towards the ground in a manoeuvre known as whiffling.

Take a closer look at a single bird among these thousands as it descends, and you can see what an extraordinary way of behaving this is. From floating in the air on outstretched wings, a bird suddenly inverts itself, sometimes momentarily flying upside down. In doing so, it turns from a perfectly balanced, aerodynamic creature into a chaotic, topsy-turvy falling object.

One theory about whiffling – and it is a very plausible one – is that the behaviour evolved to make the goose's flight pattern hard to work out, which would give it a better chance of avoiding being taken by a predator or shot by a watching wildfowler. Whatever the reason for this unusual behaviour, it makes for an incredible spectacle, especially when – as here at the RSPB's reserve on the Loch of Strathbeg – thousands of birds are descending at the same time.

When they do land there is still just enough light to make out the features that mark out the Pink-feet from their close relatives, Greylag and White-fronted Geese. These species are collectively known as grey geese, though in fact they are a dull greyish-brown in colour, with markings of white, buff and black along the edges of their feathers, which give them their distinctive 'scalloped' appearance.

One of the best ways to tell the different species of grey geese apart is to take a close look at their bills, as both the shape and colour are distinctive. Whereas the bulky Greylag Geese have a plain orange bill, and the White-fronts have a pinkish-orange one with a white patch around the base ('front' derives from the French word for forehead), the Pink-feet have a smaller, more delicate bill that is orange-pink with darker markings.

Pink-footed Geese flock to Scotland each autumn from their Arctic breeding grounds, to spend the winter here. These birds are 'whiffling' as they come into land.

The Pink-feet are also darker overall, with a contrasting pale chest, and slightly smaller than their cousins. However, the best way to tell the geese species apart is by their calls, and here the Pink-foot comes out on top, with a pleasing, almost musical sound compared with the harsh cackle of the White-fronts and the cacophonous farmyard-goose honking of the Greylags.

It's now late October and the Pink-feet have been here for almost a month. They arrived on fresh north-westerly winds in the very last days of September, having flown across the North Atlantic from their summer home in Iceland, far to the north. There they nested in steep and inaccessible river gorges, to avoid their eggs and chicks being taken by predators such as Arctic Foxes, though inevitably some youngsters are always lost, no matter how attentive their parents are.

Then, as summer turned to autumn, and the September equinox saw the hours of daylight in these high latitudes rapidly diminish, they waited for a following wind. When it came, the geese launched themselves into the air in huge, V-shaped skeins, a gathering of the clans led by the elders of the tribe, guiding the younger birds on their first ever journey south. As well as helping the youngsters find their way, flying in this formation also reduces their energy expenditure. Just as a peloton of racing cyclists enables each following competitor to save energy, so the leading goose does the lion's share of the work. The older, more experienced geese take it in turns to fly at the front, thus ensuring that the flock has the best possible chance of reaching its final destination.

Numbers of Pink-feet wintering in Britain – many of them in the Scottish Highlands and Islands – have rocketed in recent years. This is a great conservation success story, given that around 80–90 per cent of the entire world population of this attractive goose spends the winter here. At the Loch of Strathbeg there may be 80,000 Pink-footed Geese – perhaps one-fifth of all the Pink-feet in the world – so it is a relief that this site is under the safe protection of the RSPB.

Soon after dawn this huge flock of birds will rise up into the air almost as one – a sight and sound to match the evening roost – and disperse across the surrounding countryside, where the birds feed in fields of winter cereals and potatoes. As the winter goes on, they may disperse far to the south, with many using the Highland lochs and fields as a staging post before heading as far away as North Norfolk. In the spring they pass through the Highlands again, though their stay is much briefer, before heading north to breed and raise a family once more.

Britain – and especially the Highlands – are a crucial winter home for the Pink-footed Goose, with the majority of the world's population coming here.

Geese and weather forecasting

Geese are, perhaps more than any other wild creature, associated with using natural phenomena to forecast the weather. Sometimes this is linked to short-term conditions. For example, in Morayshire it was believed that if geese fly out to sea, the weather will stay fine, whereas if they head for the hills then rain is due.

Other goose-related folklore takes a longer view. For instance, large flocks of geese passing overhead in autumn are supposed to indicate that we are in for a cold winter, while the pattern of the V-shaped flock itself is somehow meant to represent the number of weeks of frost and ice that will follow later in the year.

St Martin's Day – or Martinmas – which falls on 11 November, is also linked with the migration of geese. If the weather on this day is particularly cold, this is supposed to foretell a mild winter, as in the ancient proverb: 'If the geese at Martin's Day stand on ice, they will walk in mud at Christmas.'

Another autumnal phenomenon, the sudden appearance of tiny silken spiders' webs known as gossamer floating through the air, also has a link with geese. The word gossamer derives from 'goose summer', a spell of mild weather in autumn, which often coincided with the arrival of large numbers of migratory geese.

In reality such long-term predictions are even beyond the ability of human forecasters, with their increasingly powerful supercomputers, let alone a flock of birds. What we do know is that the early or late arrival of migrating geese in autumn may be an indication of current weather conditions further north – but the birds cannot possibly predict the future, any more than we can.

MIGRATING MILLIONS

Those tens of thousands of Pink-footed Geese landing along the east coast of Scotland are not the only new arrivals from the north. All over the Highlands and Islands, from the Inner Hebrides in the west to the Moray Firth in the east, and Orkney in the north to Strathspey in the south, migrating birds are arriving in their millions.

They come here for one simple but crucial reason: to take advantage of what for us may seem like a cold winter climate, but for these Arctic creatures is mild and welcoming. Most importantly, they come to Scotland because there is plenty to eat: reliable sources of food throughout the whole of the long winter months, and (just about) enough daylight hours for them to feed.

So as well as the Pink-feet, Greylag Geese also fly here across the ocean from Iceland. Many of them stop as soon as they reach the Orkney Islands, where they can find plenty of areas to graze. Smaller, black-and-white Barnacle Geese – named after the bizarre belief that they hatched out of goose barnacles – come even further. They have travelled all the way from the High Arctic land of Spitsbergen to winter in south-west Scotland on the Solway Firth. Others fly from eastern Greenland to winter on the Isle of Mull, and elsewhere in the Highlands and Islands.

Spitsbergen, or Svalbard as it now usually known, lies at 78 degrees north, about halfway between the northernmost point of Norway and the North Pole. So to travel from here to the Highlands is the equivalent of flying all the way from Scotland to Morocco. No wonder they think Scotland's winter climate is balmy and mild!

Barnacle Geese footprints in the sand – a tangible sign of the presence of these birds, which flock to the Highlands each autumn and winter.

OVERLEAF *Whooper Swans migrate to Britain from Iceland to take advantage of our relatively mild winter climate and plenty of available food.*

The other bird of the far north to spend the winter here in the Highlands is the magnificent Whooper Swan. This rivals its cousin, the Mute Swan, for the title of Britain's largest bird, measuring up to 160 cm (63 in) long, with a wingspan of 2.3 m (7.5 ft) and weighing a whopping 9.3 kg (20 lb). Like the Pink-footed and Greylag Geese, Whooper Swans breed on the open tundra of Iceland. However, as autumn brings the first storms, snow and ice, they too head south and east towards Britain.

Like the geese they travel in family parties, the snow-white adults with their custard-yellow and black bills guiding up to eight dirty grey youngsters on this, their first migratory journey. They usually fly at a height of a few hundred feet above the ground, but in December 1967 a pilot was astonished to see a flock of Whooper Swans flying at a height of around 8,200 m (26,600 ft) above the Hebrides, still the altitude record for any British bird.

Significant Highlanders

ROY DENNIS ⋯ WILDLIFE CONSERVATIONIST

Born in the New Forest, Roy Dennis's life changed in 1959 when, as a young assistant warden on Fair Isle, he met the conservationist George Waterston, then director of RSPB Scotland. 'Operation Osprey' – the scheme to guard the Loch Garten birds against egg collectors and to show them to people – had just begun, and Waterston asked the 19-year-old if he wanted to work there the following year.

Since that first visit to Strathspey in 1960, Roy has always lived and worked in the Highlands and Islands, on an incredible range of different birds and mammals, from seabirds to Grey Seals, and wildfowl to songbirds. Yet he has always returned to his first love: Ospreys. Roy has seen incredible progress in our knowledge about these migratory, fish-eating raptors. When he first ringed a chick in 1970, the chances of ever seeing it again were almost zero. Yet by 1999 he was using tracking devices to follow the birds' journey to and from Africa. They could be erratic and the batteries didn't last long, whereas today's systems use GPS to send an accurate position of a bird every minute of the day or night during its three-week journey back to Scotland.

Today, there are at least 300 Osprey pairs in the UK, not just in Scotland but also in England – where Roy was instrumental in reintroducing them – and Wales. Red Kites and White-tailed Eagles have thrived, too. Again, Roy was in the forefront of bringing them back. Not every species has such a positive tale to tell. Roy recalls Capercaillies being so common in the forests of Strathspey that you couldn't miss them, yet today this massive grouse is almost extinct in the Highlands. He's also shocked to see the seabird declines on his beloved Fair Isle.

Roy looks back on his long career with a mixture of frustration and well-earned pride. There's frustration that real nature conservation is low in political thinking and usually takes low priority, even in the Cairngorms National Park; and pride in a life spent working closely alongside the farmers, foresters and landowners of the Highlands – the people who can carry out good wildlife management. Roy speaks of Osprey nests he has visited for over half a century, and now deals with the grandson or granddaughter of the original landowner. It's this continuity that makes his long, successful career as a conservationist unique.

LIFE IN THE FOREST

Meanwhile, away from the coast and islands, things are rather quieter. Indeed, a walk in the Caledonian pine forests at this time of year can be a dispiriting affair for a naturalist, with few sights, or even sounds, to trouble your eyes and ears. If you know where to look, however, you'll see that there is plenty of life here. Often you simply need to be patient, and use heightened senses to listen for the slightest sound – a potential clue to an exciting encounter with one of the hidden creatures of the forest.

Then, as you lift your eyes from the ground once again, a sound reaches your ears. It's almost inaudible at first, but as you approach a stand of pines it gets louder and more distinct, a light scratching and rustling, as if someone – or something – is scrabbling around in the layer of pine needles that cover the ground. And that's exactly what is happening. When you peer through the tall, vertical trunks of the pines, you notice a rapid, repetitive movement, a blur of reddish-brown shaking from side to side. As you watch, the tail (for that's what it is) drops down momentarily, to reveal a head, tufty ears and a beady black eye glancing around nervously towards you. It is a Red Squirrel, storing surplus food for a rainy – or rather a snowy – day.

Autumn is a critical time for our only native species of squirrel. In many ways it is a time of plenty, for there are plenty of pine cones on which to feed, as well as a seasonal bonus in the form of fungi, nuts and berries. However, with winter just around the corner, the squirrel's instinct tells it to prepare for what may be lean times ahead, especially a long spell of below zero temperatures, bringing ice and snow. So Red Squirrels hedge their bets by not eating everything they find. Instead they spend time 'caching' – storing food when there is plenty available by digging into the ground and hiding it.

Red Squirrels hide away food during times of plenty, so that when it snows they have something to eat.

That's a good idea in theory, but it does rely on the squirrel remembering where it hid its food supply, sometimes weeks or even months after it did so. Scientists have shown that although the squirrels have a better than even chance of finding each cache, this still means that between a third and a half of all their hidden stores either go undiscovered, or are found by other foraging birds and mammals. They have also found that Red Squirrels are not as good as the introduced Grey Squirrels at remembering exactly where their caches are – yet another factor that has enabled the Greys to win over the Reds across much of Britain.

Red Squirrels are at their most active early and late in the day, in the hours after dawn and before dusk, so these are often the best times to search for them. In winter, however, they are likely to be out and about all day, though they will retreat

The Fieldfare – a member of the thrush family – is one of our most attractive winter visitors.

to their dreys during really bad weather, when finding food can be difficult. With such high energy levels and an inability to store large reserves of fat, this does mean that they are especially vulnerable to long spells of ice and snow.

On chilly days in December it's worth keeping an eye out for these charming animals, whose russet coat seems even brighter when reflected by snow on the ground. The sight of a Red Squirrel frantically digging through the snow to search for its cache of food would be amusing, were it not for the fact that if it fails to find where it hid its food, the chances are that it will starve to death.

Other creatures survive these short winter days by cooperating. All along hedgerows and field margins throughout the Highlands, ragged flocks of birds launch into the air on late-autumn gales, battling against the wind before landing again on another hedgerow, and voraciously feeding on the remaining hawthorn berries there. They are winter thrushes: Redwings and Fieldfares that, like the geese and swans, have travelled here from the far north. The Redwings have come from Iceland and the Fieldfares from Scandinavia, a few even travelling all the way from northern Russia. A handful of Redwings and Fieldfares do breed in Scotland, mostly in the

Highlands, but the hundreds of thousands that spend the winter here dwarf this tiny breeding population.

Both species share the familiar thrush form: the larger Fieldfare is the size and shape of a Mistle Thrush, 26 cm (10 in) long and weighing about 100 g (3.5 oz); its smaller cousin is more like a Song Thrush, at 21 cm (8 in) long and weighing 63 g (2 oz).

As well as the big difference in size, the two species are also very different in appearance. Redwings are neat and compact, with a darker plumage than the Song Thrush, a pale, creamy stripe above the eye, a spotted breast, and the distinctive orange-red patch on the flanks that gives the species its common name. Fieldfares are larger, longer and rangier in appearance, with a grey head and rump, black tail, maroon back and wings, and pale yellow underparts heavily blotched with black chevrons, all finished off by a yellow bill with a black tip. Given good views, both species reveal themselves to be very attractive birds indeed.

Redwings and Fieldfares often feed together in large flocks, sometimes accompanied by small numbers of Blackbirds, or Song and Mistle Thrushes. Being in a flock has several advantages. There are more pairs of eyes to find food – mostly berries in hedgerows early in the season, and worms in fields later on – and of course to spot predators such as Sparrowhawks.

Waxwing winters

Berries are a crucial part of many birds' winter diets. But for another arrival from the north, the Waxwing, berries are not just desirable, but absolutely essential. For this reason, Waxwings are most likely to be found not in the fields and hedgerows of the open countryside, but in town gardens and even in supermarket car parks.

The Waxwing truly needs to be seen to be believed. About the size and shape of a plump Starling, it is one of the most striking of all Scotland's birds, with a reddish-brown plumage, black throat and eye-patch, wispy crest and yellow tip to the tail. What's really remarkable, however, is the Waxwing's unique wing pattern: alternating stripes of black and yellow with a small but obvious patch of red, which looks exactly like old-fashioned sealing wax – hence the bird's name.

Waxwings spend the spring and summer far to the north, in the forests of Scandinavia, up to and even beyond the Arctic Circle. In years when the berry crop is abundant, Waxwings stay put in or near the breeding areas, or perhaps head a little further afield to southern Scandinavia. But if the berry crop fails, especially when this coincides with a successful breeding season producing plenty of young, Waxwings will head much further south and west, crossing the North Sea to Britain.

The first sign that it may be a 'Waxwing winter' comes from the east coast of Scotland, where in October or November small flocks of Waxwings begin to appear, often heading straight to gardens where they gorge on the berries of exotic plants such as cotoneaster. Coming in to land they look rather like a flock of Starlings, but their distinctive plumage and unusual call – which sounds like a Trimphone from the 1980s – make them easy to recognise.

DEPTHS OF WINTER

With just four days to go before Christmas Day, the village of Braemar in the heart of Royal Deeside is thronged with shoppers, all eager to grab last-minute presents, food for the festive dinner, and even more tinsel and baubles to decorate an already overloaded tree.

Today is the winter solstice, the point on the astronomical calendar when the northern hemisphere is turned as far away as it will go from the sun, known colloquially as the shortest day. Here in the Highlands this means that the sun will not rise until almost nine o'clock in the morning, and set just after half past three in the afternoon, giving less than seven hours of daylight. Given that Braemar is nestled in a hollow between several huge, towering crags, there is little chance that the Christmas shoppers will need any suntan lotion today. Indeed, the snow is already beginning to fall, lending a suitably festive air to the proceedings.

Braemar is not quite the coldest settlement in Britain. That honour goes to the whisky-producing village of Dalwhinnie, just off the main A9 road between Perth and Inverness. However, with an average annual temperature of just 6.6° C (44 °F), it does get pretty cold here, as befits the location that has twice set the record for the lowest ever temperature recorded in the United Kingdom, a bone-chilling –27.2 °C (–17 °F).

Yet although the people of Braemar are celebrating Christmas, along with the inhabitants of towns, villages and hamlets all over the Scottish Highlands, for the region's wildlife winter has only just begun. From now on the days will gradually lengthen, until on 21 March – the spring equinox – there will 12 hours of daylight and 12 hours of night both here and everywhere else on the planet. However, the mercury will continue to stay below or close to freezing throughout January and February, and often well into March. As well as the low temperatures, Highland wildlife will also have to cope with snow and ice, which make finding food difficult – perhaps even impossible.

When the landscape begins to ice over in the middle of winter, many wild creatures will struggle to survive, usually because it is harder to find food.

Golden Eagles must hunt throughout the short daylight hours during the depths of winter, so this is a good time to see them on the wing.

Yet none of this bothers one mighty Highland predator. The Golden Eagle perched on a crag high above the valley below has no qualms about the temperature dropping, or the falling snow. She welcomes the winter – for her, it just makes it easier to hunt for food, or to scavenge the carcasses of dead and dying animals such as sheep and deer; creatures for which the recent snowfalls have proved the final straw, leaving them too weak to feed.

Today, however, the eagle is not scavenging, but hunting; as she glides across the snow-covered slopes she searches the land below with her incredibly sharp eyes. Her quarry? Mountain Hares. A small group of these animals crouches low in the lee of a huge granite boulder, ears pushed back and bodies hunched as they try to shelter from the biting north-westerly wind. They have fluffed out their greyish-white fur to try to preserve as much heat as they can, so that they look rather like small rocks – until, that is, one hare scents something on the wind and twitches its nose to discover more.

Another hare – a youngster, born the previous spring and less experienced than its fellow creatures – loses patience, and decides to venture out to forage for food. His impetuosity may prove fatal, for just as he lollops slowly across the snowfield, the eagle appears low over the crest of the mountain slope. Alert to any movement in this otherwise motionless scene, the eagle notices the hare out of the corner of her eye. She lifts her left wing imperceptibly, just enough to slow down and change direction. Then she folds both wings in towards her body and begins to drop down towards her target.

Meanwhile, the hare itself has somehow divined the eagle's presence; looking up, he sees a dark shape etched against the snowy hillside. Instinct tells him one thing – to run – so he draws his powerful hind legs up towards his body and launches himself rapidly downhill, zigzagging from side to side in order to maximise his chances of escaping the eagle's claws.

Above, the eagle follows every twist and turn – and as she gets closer and closer she extends her feathered legs, each ending in a fearsome set of talons, and prepares to go in for the kill. Three metres... two metres... one metre... surely the hare has only moments to live...

Then, at the very last moment, a shape appears along the gully to the side of the action: a human figure, clad in bright red, muffled against the cold, and carrying two sharp sticks. It's a skier braving the bitter cold on the slopes of the mountain.

The eagle has only one instinct greater than that to

hunt and kill, and that is to survive. To Golden Eagles, after centuries of persecution a human being means only one thing: danger. So just milliseconds before her claws would have sunk into the hare's flesh, she draws them back, flaps her wings and flies away as quickly as she can. The hare lies shaking in the snow, unable to comprehend how it can still be alive. The skier continues downhill, unaware of the drama he has left behind.

Another creature has not been quite so lucky. The old Red Deer stag, wandering aimlessly after losing his place as the king of the deer rut back in October, has finally given up the fight to live. Today, he is making his last climb, up a stream along one of the gullies that run down the mountainside, trudging steadily uphill through the snow.

There, unseen by animal or human eyes, he crouches down on his knees, slumps to one side, and as night falls, exhales his final breath, a small cloud of mist that evaporates unseen on the December air. At more than 20 years old he has had a pretty good run, siring dozens, perhaps hundreds of offspring. Now they are the only evidence of his presence on this Earth, apart from his rapidly stiffening corpse.

By the time morning comes the night frost has left a thin coat of white across his antlers, head and body, as if he is melting back into the winter landscape itself. But for him, the hours and days after his death will not be peaceful, for his carcass will soon provide food for the clean-up squad of the mountains.

First to arrive, in the hour after dawn, is a Hooded Crow. This is the northern equivalent of the more widespread Carrion Crow, found mainly north and west of the Great Glen. Hoodies, as they are often called, are easily told apart from their southern relatives by their grey upper back and belly, contrasting with the jet-black head, breast, wings and tail. He lands awkwardly by the deer's corpse, tentatively checking that the animal really is dead. Then he hops up onto the animal's back and begins pecking at the hide with his beak. Soon he is joined by another, and then another – but despite their collective efforts the old deer's skin is still far too tough for them to pierce, however hard they try.

A shadow briefly crosses the deer carcass – looking up, the Hooded Crows react nervously and hop a few feet away. The shadow materialises into a Raven. Weighing around 1.3 kg (3 lb) and with a wingspan of more than 1.3 m (4 ft) this all-black bird is the largest and most fearsome member of the crow family. He is in charge, and he knows it.

The Raven is an old male, hatched out ten years earlier in the forests of the valley below. Unlike the

Red Deer stags are the most magnificent creatures of the whole of the Scottish Highlands. They are well able to cope with the worst of the winter weather.

young Hoodies, he has scavenged many a deer corpse before, and he knows that the easiest way in is to start with the soft parts: the black, lifeless eyes, or the fleshy belly. Hopping onto the stag's antlers, he leans forwards and with a practised blow sinks his huge, jet-black beak into the animal's right eye, drawing it out to leave a messy red hole in the socket. The left side of the stag's face is pressed against the ground, so after this tasty but unsatisfying hors d'oeuvre, the Raven moves onto the main course.

The stag's belly may be soft, but it is still covered with a surprisingly thick layer of hair and skin. The Raven needs help, so he lifts his head and utters a call so deep that it echoes round the gully, a sound that seems to rise up from the very belly of the Earth. Excitedly, the Hooded Crows join in, adding a descant of loud, harsh 'konk, konk' calls to the Raven's deep, resonant croak.

The signal works almost immediately: from every side, little flocks of Hooded Crows and single Ravens begin to arrive. The Hoodies stand on the sidelines as the Ravens get to work, pecking relentlessly at the deer's belly until, eventually, one succeeds in piercing the hide and a slow trickle of deep crimson blood begins to ooze out onto the snow.

The sight and smell of the blood acts like a trigger to the Ravens. Frantically they jostle one another, flapping their huge wings to drive their rivals out of the way so they can get to the fleshy guts of the dead stag. For the next hour or two, as the winter sun creeps higher and higher in the sky, they tear, stab and rip the deer's flesh, spilling its entrails out onto the ground until the scene begins to resemble a fight in an abattoir.

From time to time a Hooded Crow leaps in and grabs a morsel – but for now at least, the bigger Ravens are completely dominant. Until, that is, an even larger and fiercer bird arrives on the scene. The big female Golden Eagle, still hungry after being frustrated by that passing skier, has noticed the sight and sounds of the crows' commotion, and has come to investigate. Her arrival causes consternation; even a Raven is no match for a bird weighing more than four times as much at it does. Discretion proves the better part of valour, and the Ravens pecking at the deer's carcass hop rapidly aside, leaving the field open for the mighty eagle.

She feeds rapidly but nervously, constantly lifting her head and glancing from side to side to make sure that this time no human will disturb her. It takes her more than three hours to have her fill, by which time there is barely half an hour of daylight left for the Ravens and Hoodies to feed. As the eagle lumbers slowly to one side, her belly so full that she can barely move, the other birds throng hastily around what remains of the deer and gorge themselves on its rapidly freezing flesh.

The eagle may feel too full to move, but she must rouse herself and get to her roost on a craggy outcrop before night falls. She half runs, half hops forwards, frantically flapping her wings until she finally lifts her weight – along with several kilos of deer flesh in her stomach – into the air, before vanishing over the silhouette of the mountain ridge. Soon afterwards the Ravens and Hoodies follow, their harsh, echoing cries fading away into the growing darkness as they descend the slopes to the black, forbidding forests below.

Few creatures do quite so well in winter as the Golden Eagle, which can take advantage of the glut of available carrion to feed.

SARAH PERN ⋯ DOLPHIN GUIDE

Sarah Pern has enjoyed 'messing about in boats' since before she was even able to walk. Raised in Cromarty, her father was a lobster fisherman before he retrained as a doctor, so boats and the sea were a huge part of Sarah's childhood.

After training as a naval architect and small craft engineer, Sarah spent some years sailing around the globe, visiting such remote and spectacular places as Antarctica, South Georgia, Tierra del Fuego and the Falkland Islands. However, her heart has always been in the Highlands – a place she always knew she would return to. It's hardly surprising, then, that she now spends her time taking visitors out on her boat around the Moray Firth for her own company, EcoVentures, which she set up more than a decade ago.

The seasons and the weather play a huge part in Sarah's life, especially during the busy summer tourist period. Her favourite time of year is the spring, when longer days with more settled weather allow her more time out on the water, just at the time when the seabird colonies and dolphins start to become more active.

She thinks that the reason she's still doing what she does is that she never quite knows what she'll find when she leaves the harbour. When she takes visitors out on the water, sometimes all they'll see is a distant glimpse of a disappearing tail, but at other times they might enjoy a once in a lifetime moment, such as coming across a pod of Pilot Whales or Basking Sharks, seemingly out of nowhere.

For Sarah, the land is just as important as the sea: especially her home patch on the Black Isle. She loves the fact that the Highlands, despite being such a small area, offers such a variety of habitats to explore. Within an hour's drive of the rolling, fertile Black Isle farmland you can be high on the hills, surrounded by rugged mountain scenery with only eagles and Red Deer for company.

What Sarah enjoys the most, however, is showing this wonderful wildlife to visitors. Sometimes she has to pinch herself to realise that seeing dolphins while waiting for a bus or walking the children to school really is something special. Only when she sees it through the eyes of people who have never seen a wild dolphin before, and witnesses their enjoyment and wonder, does she realise just how special an experience this is.

OUT WITH THE OLD...

On New Year's Eve, the sun doesn't usually appear above the slopes of Cairn Gorm until the middle of the morning. Today, however, on the very last day of an eventful year, the sun isn't going to appear at all. The sky is the shade of a battleship, the wind is strengthening, and the weather forecasters are predicting a blizzard to see out the old year and bring in the new.

Snow begins to fall around lunchtime, the wind is gusting at close to a hundred miles an hour, and by 2 p.m. the skiers and hikers have all come off the mountain, either because they have heard the weather forecast, or because they need time to prepare for the festivities ahead. For tonight is Hogmanay, and all over the Scottish Highlands foaming glasses of beer and drams of the finest malt whisky will be raised to see in the New Year.

Below the summit of Cairn Gorm itself, the Ptarmigan Restaurant closes its doors. For now at least, the little flock of Snow Buntings will have to forage for food without a helping hand from humans. The funicular railway and ski lifts have also closed; no sensible person wants to be out and about on the mountain in such terrible conditions. No such comfort is available to the wild residents of the high tops, though. Whatever the weather, they must find a way to survive here for 365 days a year, and for 24 hours every day, and night.

As dusk begins to fall, the blizzard intensifies. Now the snow is almost horizontal, sweeping in great flurries not just through the air, but off the slopes of the mountain too, whipped up by the strengthening gusts of wind. For the Ptarmigans it's time to find shelter, which they do by digging down into the soft layer of snow using their feathered feet, then wriggling their bodies inside this makeshift igloo, a natural duvet that will keep them warm – or at least warm enough to survive.

Apart from a yellow patch of lichen, this winter landscape on the high tops of the Cairnwell Summit, Glenshee, looks bleak and entirely lifeless.

The Mountain Hares have sought shelter too, huddling together in a small group just beneath the lip of a protruding rock facing away from the wind, where the worst of the snow does not enter. Even the Stoats – the toughest little animal of all – have fled, heading downhill to seek shelter in the pine forests of the valley below.

Only one creature remains in view. It's one animal for whom these blizzard conditions are simply normal, and which is so well adapted to life here on the high tops that it simply forms a close-knit herd that stands together, waiting for the New Year's Eve storm to blow itself out – the Reindeer. Anyone reckless enough to risk venturing out on the Cairngorm plateau today would no doubt be impressed by the sheer stoicism of these amazing animals. They did, after all, evolve to live beyond the Arctic Circle, and no other creature is quite as well adapted to life in the cold. So when the blizzard comes, they simply huddle together to protect their youngsters, and rely on their incredible adaptations to survive until the wind blows itself out.

The Cairngorm Reindeer could hardly be better suited to this harsh environment – especially when it snows.

AND IN WITH THE NEW...

The storm does, eventually, end. In the hours before dawn on New Year's Day, just as hundreds of partygoers are staggering back home in nearby Braemar, Aviemore and Grantown-on-Spey, the weather system that brought the blizzard first weakens, then finally slips away towards the east.

As another year begins we can look back on the past 12 months. Nature's calendar has completed its full cycle here in the Highlands: a cycle of courtship and nest building, emergence and growth, mating and raising families, fighting and winning – and for some, losing – and of course killing and being killed. Those that died have, hopefully, left their legacy in their offspring; those that have managed to survive have another year to look forward to – as have we.

It's been a year of four seasons, each of which blurs gradually but inexorably into the next. They are seasons full of joys and wonders, horrors and delights, hopes and fears – both for the wildlife of this unique and precious region of the British Isles, and for us.

And so, as the sun finally rises over the summit of Cairn Gorm on the first day of the New Year, and the first hardy skiers head up the mountain, down in the valley below a bird hops onto the top of a Scots Pine and begins to call. For the Scottish Crossbill – the only wild creature unique to the Scottish Highlands – spring has already begun.

A tiny Scots Pine begins its long journey growing into a mighty tree so characteristic of the Scottish Highlands.

ACKNOWLEDGEMENTS

This book accompanies the BBC TV series *Highlands – Scotland's Wild Heart*, made by the Glasgow-based independent production company Maramedia. I should particularly like to thank Maramedia's main man Nigel Pope. Nigel has been a friend and colleague for many years now, since we both worked together at the BBC Natural History Unit in Bristol, on pioneering series such as *Big Cat Diary* and *Springwatch*. It was he who kindly suggested that I write this book, and he has also masterminded the truly excellent series that it accompanies. Also at Maramedia, I'd like to thank Jackie Savery, Carol Davidson, Simon Williams, Justin Purefoy, Amy Thompson and Fergus Gill, and also Lindsay McCrae and Raymond Besant, the two brilliant young series cameramen.

The book was commissioned by Bloomsbury who, under its former natural history editor Nigel Redman, has established an unparalleled record in wildlife publishing. I owe a huge debt of thanks to Julie Bailey, under whose expert eye the book has progressed from an idea to the finished article; and also to her designer, Nicola Liddiard at Nimbus Design, for the book's stunning design. My agent, Broo Doherty, was her usual unflappable self throughout.

My dear friend John Lister-Kaye – no mean author himself – has read over the chapters and made many helpful suggestions and corrections – any errors that may remain are of course my own. John is one of the ten men and women who kindly agreed to appear in the book. Thanks also go to the others: Gordon Buchanan, Laurie Campbell, Peter Cunningham, Roy Dennis, Sarah Pern, David Sexton, Fiona Smith, Evelyn Spence and Jonathan Willet. They represent just a flavour of the many passionate and knowledgeable people who have hugely contributed to the Highlands and their wildlife.

Anyone writing about the Highlands must also acknowledge those who have gone before: giants of conservation, sadly no longer with us, such as Frank Fraser Darling, John Morton Boyd, Desmond Nethersole-Thompson and Dick Balharry; and those who still are, such as the incomparable Adam Watson, with whom I had the pleasure of climbing up Glen Shee in search of Ptarmigan and Dotterel almost 20 years ago.

Finally, this book would be far less striking without the stunning photographs of Laurie Campbell. Laurie is the greatest of many fine wildlife photographers based in Scotland: his sheer dedication, amazing skill and acute eye for capturing the natural world in all its decisive moments is, quite simply, unparalleled.

FURTHER READING

Travel and Wildlife Guides

Lonely Planet Scotland's Highlands and Islands
(Lonely Planet, 2015)

The Rough Guide to Scottish Highlands and Islands
(Rough Guides, 2014)

Best Birdwatching Sites: Scottish Highlands,
by Gordon Hamlett (Buckingham Press, 2014)

Environment and Conservation

The Changing Nature of Scotland, various editors
(TSO Scotland, 2011)

The Nature of the Cairngorms: Diversity in a changing environment, edited by Philip Shaw and Des Thompson
(TSO Scotland, 2006)

Contested Mountains, by Robert A. Lambert
(The White Horse Press, 2001)

History and Culture

Scottish Birds: Culture and Tradition, by Robin Hull
(Mercat Press, 2001)

Scottish Mammals, by Robin Hull (Birlinn, 2007)

A Guide to Scots Bird Names, by Robin Jackson
(Ptarmigan Press, 2013)

Fauna Scotica: People and Animals in Scotland,
by Polly Pullar and Mary Low (Birlinn, 2012)

Flora Celtica: Plants and People in Scotland, by
William Milliken (Birlinn, 2013)

The Ancient Pinewoods of Scotland, by Clifton Bain
(Sandstone Press, 2013)

Nature Writing

Song of the Rolling Earth: a Highland Odyssey,
by John Lister-Kaye (Time Warner, 2003)

Gods of the Morning: A Bird's Eye View of a Highland Year, by John Lister-Kaye (Canongate, 2015)

PHOTOGRAPH CREDITS

With the exception of those on the page numbers below, Laurie Campbell took all the photographs in this book. Bloomsbury Publishing would like to thank Laurie and all those named below for providing photographs and for permission to reproduce copyright material within this book.

26 © Gordon Buchanan; 39 © Paul Hobson/FLPA; 55 © Justin Purefoy; 98 © John Paul; 122 © Richard Taylor-Jones; 144 © Warwick Lister-Kaye; 148 © Graham Munton; 170 all © Jonathan Willet; 179 © Hugh Harrop; 189 © Colin Riach; 224 top © Ben Rushbrooke; 244 © Peter Cairns; 250 © EcoVentures, Cromarty.

A

Abernethy Forest **123**
Adder **87, 145**
Admiral, Red **146**
Aigas Field Centre,
　Beauly **53, 145, 171**
Arctic-Alpine ecosystems
　16
Ardnamurchan Peninsula
　27
Argus, Scotch **149,
184–187**
Auk, Great **116**
Aviemore **266**

B

Badger **46**
Banchory **74**
Bear, Brown **56**
Beauly **53, 74, 145, 190**
Bedstraw, Heath **149**
Beetle, Great Diving **163**
Beinn Eighe National
　Nature Reserve **171,
209**
Ben Lawers **146**
Ben Macdui **21**
Bilberry **149**
birdsong **74–77**
Black Isle, Moray Firth
　171, 204, 261
Blackbird **74, 247**
Blackcap **77**
Boat of Garten **74**
Bonxie **119–120**
Braemar **16, 74, 250,
266**
Brambling **43–45**
Bridge of Grudie **193**
Buchanan, Gordon
　122–123

Bunting, Snow **28–31,
99, 262**
butterflies **71 , 146**
　Chequered Skipper
　150–151
　Large Heath **163**
　Mountain Ringlet
　146–150, 187
　Scotch Argus **149,
184–187**
Buzzard, Common **31**

C

Cairngorms **21, 99, 123,
159–160, 243**
　Cairn Gorm **12, 16, 28,
262, 266**
　plateau **60, 80, 116,
136, 202, 264**
　weather and climate **16**
Caledonian Forest **36,
60, 123**
Caledonian pine forests
　**60–61, 74, 90, 100, 116,
123, 184, 244**
Callanish, Lewis **156, 158**
Campbell, Laurie
　208–209
Capercaillie **60, 90,
92–95, 171, 243**
Caribou **12**
cats, feral **40, 56–59**
Chaffinch **34, 40–43**
Chanonry Point, Moray
　Firth **176**
Chaser, Four-spotted
　190
Chiffchaff **77**
Coire Loch **190**
Copinsay **212**
Corncrake **134–136**
Creag Meagaidh **146**

Crex crex **134**
Cromarty, Moray Firth
　261
Crossbill, Common **38**
　Parrot **38**
　Scottish **34–39, 46, 60,
96, 266**
Crow, Carrion **254**
　Hooded **93, 254–258**
Cuckoo **68, 71, 133, 152**
Cunningham, Peter
　224–225

D

Dalwhinnie **250**
damselflies **71, 171,
190–195**
Damselfly, Common Blue
　190, 193
　Emerald **190, 193–195**
　Northern Emerald **171,
192–194**
Darter, Black **193**
　Common **193**
　Highland **193**
　White-faced **193**
Deer, Red **27, 93–94, 171,
198–201, 209, 218, 223,
225, 254, 261**
　Roe **55**
Deeside **38, 44, 74,
250**
Dennis, Roy **127,
242–243**
Dipper **115, 226**
Diver, Black-throated **65,
160, 165–169**
　Great Northern **65**
　Red-throated **65, 165**
divers **62–65**
Dolphin, Bottlenose
　176–178

Dotterel **68, 136–137,
140, 204**
dragonflies **71, 171,
190–195**
Dragonfly, Golden-ringed
　193
Duck, Long-tailed **207**
Dunlin **160, 169, 196,
207**

E

Eagle, Golden **22, 27–33,
80–84, 108, 124, 143,
145, 171, 202, 209,
253–259**
　Cainism **143**
　nesting **80–83**
Eagle, White-tailed **27,
111, 124, 243**
EcoVentures **261**
Eider, Common **65, 207**
Elizabeth II **12**
Emerald, Brilliant
　193–194
　Downy **194**
　Northern **171, 192–194**
Ermine **25**
Eynhallow, Orkneys
　180–183

F

Fair Isle **243**
Felis sylvestris **56**
　grampia **56**
Fieldfare **246–247**
Flow Country **65, 152,
159, 160–163, 166**
　forestry **164**
Fly Agaric **152**

Flycatcher, Spotted **133,
204**
Forestry Commission **93**
Fox, Arctic **234**
　Red **46**
Fraserburgh **65**
Frog, Common **87**
Fulmar **119, 172–174, 180**

G

Gairloch **225**
geese and weather
　forecasting **236**
Glen Affric **190, 193**
Godwit **207**
Goldcrest **44, 76–77, 185**
Goldeneye **102–105, 205**
Goldfinch **74**
Goose, Barnacle **207, 238**
　Greylag **232, 234, 238,
240**
　Pink-footed **65,
232–238, 240**
　White-fronted **207, 232,
234**
Grantown-on-Spey **202,
266**
Great Glen **44, 80, 152,
254**
Grebe, Black-necked **78**
　Great Crested **78**
　Little **78**
　Slavonian **62–63, 78–79**
Greenfinch **43, 74**
Greenshank **160, 169**
Grey Seals Protection Act
　1914 **218**
grouse shooting **196**
Grouse, Black **60, 94–95,
96**
　Red **21, 32, 38, 196**

Willow **38, 196**
Guillemot **78, 116, 120,
172**
　Black **180**
Gull, Great Black-backed
　120, 174
　Herring **119**

H

Hare, Brown **22**
　Mountain **18, 20, 22–25,
28, 32, 80, 84–87, 140,
202, 253, 264**
Harrier, Hen **160, 196**
Hawfinch **34**
Hawker, Azure **171,
193–194**
　Common **191**
　Southern **190**
Heath, Large **163**
Hebrides **152, 156, 238,
240**
Hedgehog **71**
Heron **230**
Highland Council **171**
Hobby **68**
Honey-buzzard **68**
Howerd, Frankie **65**

I

Islay **160**

K

Kite, Red **243**
Kittiwake **119–120, 172,
174**
Knot **152, 207**

L

Landrail **134**
Lapwing **145**
Larch **34**
lekking **94**
Lindgren, Ethel **12**
Lister-Kaye, John **144–145**
Loch Garten **43–44, 124–129, 193, 204, 243**
Loch Loyne **127**
Loch Maree **193**
Loch Ness **71, 188–189**
Loch of Strathbeg **65, 232–234**
Loch Ruthven **78**
Lutra lutra **108**
Lynx, Eurasian **56**

M

Mallard **65**
marine life **176–183, 212–223**
Marten, Pine **27, 46, 50–53, 56, 60, 93, 96, 145, 171, 209**
breeding **101–103**
Martin, House **130, 204**
Maxwell, Gavin *Ring of Bright Water* **111, 145**
McKenna, Virginia **111**
Merlin **160, 169, 196**
Midge, Highland **198, 225**
migrating birds **68–71, 130–133, 159, 204–207, 238–241**
geese and weather forecasting **236**
Monach Isles **212**
Moor-grass, Purple **184**
Moorhen **134**

Moray Firth **44, 212, 238**
moths **71**
Mouse, Field **55**
Mull, Isle of **27, 123, 159–160, 238**
Mustela erminea **25**

N

Nairn **74**
Nethy Bridge **74, 112, 204**

O

Oddie, Bill **127**
Operation Osprey **125, 241**
Orca **178–179**
Orkney **156–159, 166, 178, 180, 238**
Osprey **68, 77, 124–130, 204, 243**
Otter **108–111, 230**
Sea **108**
Smooth-coated **111**
Oystercatcher **207**

P

Peregrine **174**
Pern, Sarah **260–261**
Peterhead **65**
Pike **78**
Pine, Lodgepole **34**
Scots **34, 60, 100, 225, 266–267**
Pipit, Meadow **133, 152, 169**
Pliny the Elder **60**
Plover, Golden **160, 196**
Porpoise, Harbour **176**

Ptarmigan **18–22, 25, 28, 32, 84–87, 123, 140, 202, 262**
Willow **38**
Puffin **71, 119–120, 136, 174–175, 180**

R

Rabbit **22, 53, 143, 174**
Rail, Water **134**
Ransome, Arthur *Great Northern?* **65**
Raven **254–258**
Razorbill **78, 116, 120–121, 172–173**
Red Kite Tours **171**
Redstart **204**
Redwing **247**
Reindeer **12–14, 22, 98–99, 202, 264–265**
Ringlet, Mountain **146–150, 187**
River Dee **108, 116, 230**
River Spey **108, 112, 116, 230**
Rogie Falls, Black Water **226**
RSPB **27, 43, 65, 78, 127, 134, 163–164, 232, 234, 243**

S

Salmon, Atlantic **71, 223, 224–27**
life cycle **228–29**
Sandaig Bay **109**
Sanderling **207**
Sandpiper, Common **68–69, 71, 115**
Green **68, 152**
Wood **68**

Scoter, Common **65, 160**
Velvet **65**
seabirds **116–121, 172–175**
Seal, Atlantic Grey **180–183, 212–223, 226, 243**
breeding **212–223**
infanticide **223**
Seal, Common/Harbour **180–183, 218**
Horsehead **218**
Sexton, David **26–27**
Shark, Basking **27, 225, 261**
Shetland **160, 166**
Sibbald, Sir Robert **21**
Siskin **42–43**
Skipper, Chequered **150–151**
Skua, Arctic **117, 118, 173, 178**
Great **117–18, 178**
Skylark **169**
Smith, Fiona **98–99**
Spaniel, Cocker **213**
Sparrow, House **40**
Sparrowhawk **40, 247**
Spence, Evelyn **54–55**
Speyside **43, 110–13, 116, 150, 160, 193, 204**
Spey Valley **74, 124, 136**
Spruce, Norway **164**
Sitka **34, 93, 164**
Squirrel, Grey **46–49, 50, 246**
Persian **46**
Squirrel, Red **46–49, 50, 53, 60, 96, 145, 171, 244–247**
breeding **100–101**
Starling **115, 248**
Stenness, Orkney **156**
Stoat **18, 22, 25, 28, 46, 50, 84–87, 103, 140, 202, 264**

Stonehenge, Salisbury Plain **156**
Strathspey **44, 107, 159, 238, 243**
Sundew **162–163**
Swallow **71, 130, 204–205**
Swan, Bewick's **207**
Mute **240**
Whooper **65, 207, 240–241**
Swift **130**

T

Tern, Arctic **180**
Thomas, Jeremy **144**
Thrush, Mistle **247**
Song **74, 247**
Tit, Blue **43, 44, 130**
Coal **43, 44, 77, 187**
Crested **44–45, 46, 60, 77, 100, 103, 171, 187**
breeding **96–97**
Tit, Great **43, 44, 74**
Tormentil **149**
Tortoiseshell, Small **146**
Travers, Bill **111**
Treecreeper **44, 77**
Trees for Life **123**
Trout, Brown **188, 225**
ferox **71, 188**
Rainbow **128**
Sea **225**
Turnstone **207**
Tystie **180**

U

UNESCO World Heritage Site **164**
Utsi, Mikel **12**

W

waders **206–207**
Wagtail, Grey **112–115, 226**
Yellow **112**
Warbler, Sedge **204**
Willow **77, 130–133, 136**
Wood **133**
Wasp, Horntail Wood **145**
waterbirds **62–67**
Waterston, George **127, 243**
Watson, Jeff **143**
Waxwing **248–249**
Weasel **46, 50, 145**
Wester Ross Fisheries Trust **225**
Western Isles **160**
Whale, Killer **178–179**
Minke **27, 225**
Pilot **261**
Wheatear **130–131**
Whinchat **133, 204**
Wildcat, Scottish **46, 56–59, 60, 108**
breeding **103**
Willet, Jonathan **170–171**
Wolf, Grey **56**
Woodcock **94**
Wren **74, 115**

Y

Ythan Estuary **152, 207**